W9-BVX-859

TEEN Empower POWER

Solid Gold Advice for Those Who Teach, Lead & Guide Today's Teens from America's Top Speakers and Authors In Education

Clare LaMeres ▪ Milton Creagh ▪ Eric Chester
John Crudele ▪ Sandy Queen ▪ Scott Friedman
Jimmy Cabrera ▪ Bill Cordes ▪ C. Kevin Wanzer
Bobby Petrocelli ▪ Ty Sells ▪ Bob Lenz
and Michael Scott Karpovich

Compiled by
Eric Chester

Copyright © MCMXCVII

Printed by Patterson Printing, Benton Harbor, Michigan

Cover design and layout by Ad Graphics, Tulsa, Oklahoma
(800) 368-6196

Library of Congress Catalog Card Number: 97-065415

ISBN: 0-9651447-2-0

TEEN POWER™
TEEN POWER TOO™
PreTEEN POWER™
TEEN EmPOWER™
are registered trademarks of ChesPress Publications

Published by:

ChesPress Publications
a subsidiary of Chester Performance Systems
1410 Vance St., Suite 201
Lakewood, CO 80215
(303)239-9999

Additional copies of
TEEN EmPOWER
can be obtained from any of the authors.
Contact information is at the end of the book.

Quantity discounts are available.

Web Site: www.teenpower.com

Contents

Where the authors are from, by chapter number

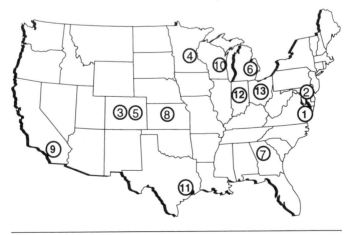

Introduction

Those of you reading this book share a common interest with its authors. You obviously have a concern for the future of this planet and a commitment to grooming its future leaders. Whether you are a parent, educator, employer, coach, counselor, activity advisor/sponsor (or perhaps all of the above), you are in the "teen business." A demanding enterprise, to be sure!

A business used to be able to stay afloat if it followed a simple principle: *buy for a buck and sell for two.* For a business to survive today, it must have (and follow) a strategic business plan. Similarly, teenagers used to do what they were told. To motivate a teen today, you must have (and follow) a strategic plan. Teen EmPower has been designed to be an integral part of your strategic plan for teaching, leading, and guiding the teens of a new generation. A combined effort of thirteen of America's most heralded teen empowerers, this book offers both the creative ideas and the practical strategies for strengthening, inspiring, and motivating today's youth.

Some stories in this book will make you laugh and others will bring a tear to your eye. You might relate to one chapter but feel somewhat removed from another. That's the beauty of this format – what you read depends on what appeals to you. Use the ideas and philosophies that apply to your unique teen interactions. If you feel a connection to one of the authors, the last section will tell you how to contact them directly.

So go ahead! Pick a chapter, any chapter, and open your mind to endless possibilities and proven strategies for empowering teens. I guarantee you will discover new and exciting ways of touching young hearts, piercing young minds, and sculpting young souls.

Happy EmPowering!

Your "business partner,"
Eric Chester

Making a Difference...
10 Seconds at a Time!

by
BOBBY PETROCELLI

TEEN
POWER

Making a Difference...
10 Seconds at a Time!

by
BOBBY PETROCELLI

"Good and evil increase at compound interest.
That is why the <u>little decisions</u> you and I make
<u>every day</u> are of such <u>infinite importance</u>."
— *C. S. Lewis*

This is one of my favorite quotes to live by. People fail to realize that every decision is significant. They not only effect the one making the decision, but ultimately touches everyone. Reaping positive benefits or facing negative consequences are direct results of decisions that are continuously made. It is easier to "stay out of trouble" than to "get out of trouble." A person can do something in an instant that can bring either great joy or heartache for a lifetime. Each person is building their own life's foundation. Choices determine which brick is placed into their foundation.

Adults can have the greatest influence in the lives of young people. Choices made during adolescence will have long-term benefits or consequences. In the business world, salesmen know if a customer doesn't buy their products, the customer will go elsewhere. Children need to feel safe, wanted and loved. They need an adults love, respect and knowledge of life. Love is a great investment. No matter whom you give it to, it returns great dividends. If a child is not getting the love and attention from the adults in their life, they will go somewhere else to find it.

Teens want attention and will go to extreme lengths to get it. Regardless of age or color, we all need love. We can't expect them to listen to our advice and ignore our example. If love is not taught in the home, it is more difficult to learn elsewhere. In every face to face encounter, regardless of how brief, we leave something behind. If you want to do something positive for youth, work on improving your life so that your actions speak for themselves. Young people are <u>always</u> watching us.

What children learn at home and from influential adults, will stay with them. Kids seek the approval and appreciation of their parents. I know, I still do. Education, experience and memories can never be taken from us. Even though it may not seem true, children secretly are glad when adults are strict and expect them to be responsible. Discipline is not a dirty word. If I ever got in trouble at school, I would be in more trouble when I got home. A strong code of ethics for young people can be as valuable to them as a compass is for a traveler.

Don't look back at the "I never got around to do List." Ask any older adult the question, "If you had to live life over again, what would you do differently?" The majority contend that spending more time and effort on the personal and professional relationships is essential. Teenage years are comprised of tribulation, confusion, agony and love. Successful adults do all they can to enhance strong foundations in the lives of young people.

On The Road Of Life
There Are No Rest Areas!

When I travel I frequently stop at rest areas to take breaks. Though I am taking a break, time and traffic march on. **WE CAN TAKE A BREAK IN OUR LIFE BUT WE CAN'T TAKE A BREAK FROM LIFE!** We are in the "Game of Life." There is no spring training, dress rehearsal or exhibition games. Nothing of value comes without effort. Success is more often the result of hard work than of talent. Self-confidence greatly determines success. To be successful with young people means taking chances. Successful people continually work on becoming the best that they can be. They are constantly practicing. We have heard the expression, "Practice makes perfect." I like the expression, **"PRACTICE MAKES PERMANENT."** "How do you get to Carneige Hall?" Practice! Practice! Practice! _It is easier to keep up than to catch up!_

It Is, Has Been And Will Always Be The Little Things That Make The Greatest Difference!

The simple things are often the most satisfying or detrimental. Serving our fellow man is the greatest gift that we can give to our world. **WHEN WE MAKE A DIFFERNCE IN ONE LIFE, WE ARE MAKING A DIFFERENCE IN OUR WORLD.** If we pursue happiness, it will elude us. But if we focus on our family, the needs of others, our call in life, meeting new people, and doing the best we can, happiness will find us. It shows when we care. Our society seems to focus it's attention on a person's outer appearance. Real attractiveness is a positive, caring attitude.

Enthusiasm is caught, not taught. It doesn't cost us anything to be nice. You will never regret being too generous, but often regret not being generous enough. **BE GENEROUS WITH PRAISE.** Keep their spirit open. Nourish their spirit. Like the phone company advertisement says, **"Reach out and touch someone."** People love human touch like holding hands, a warm hug or even a pat on the back. Kids need hugs more than they need things. Kids can never be loved, praised or hugged too much. Getting caught up in self pity would be waste of time. When I have pains, it does not grant me permission to be a pain. You may be that young person's most important role model. Encourage youth to be **"on the attack"** instead of **"under attack"** as they face the challenges of this world.

"Nothing splendid has ever been achieved except by those who believed that something inside of them was superior to circumstances."
— *Bruce Barton*

Every choice we make sets patterns, habits, routines and practices in our lives. We are building foundations – 1 brick, 1 decision at a time. *We shouldn't expect life's very best, if we are not giving our best.* **PHYSICIAN HEAL THYSELF.** If we let our problems rule our life, we lose our effectiveness. Our priorities need to be in order. Children learn from example. *Throw out the saying, "Do as I say, not as I do."* As role models we need to be loving. Even if it is hard to forget, we still need to **_FORGIVE_**. The three greatest words you can say are, "I forgive you."

When people plot revenge, they allow the person who has already hurt them, to hurt them longer. We are never in control of how others treat us, but we are in control of how we act, react and respond to the situation. I am so very thankful that I never let the drunk driver who killed my wife (while we were asleep in bed – he crashed his full size pick-up truck through my brick bedroom wall) hurt me a second time. Choosing to hate and be unforgiving would have been the greatest tragedy of all. I would have cheated life. Today, because of my foundation, habits, practices and routines, I have been able to go on with my life. I have been remarried (Suzanne Marie) and have two of the most wonderful sons (Alec and Aron). I also have traveled sharing my **Triumph over Tragedy** and **10 seconds can change lives forever** worldwide. The lives I have had the **HONOR** and **PRIVILEGE** of touching may never have been touched. I thank **God daily** that I didn't give up.

"It's not what happens to you,
it's what you do about it."
— *W. Mitchell*

We need to treasure children for who they are. Encouragement can turn a child around. Become familiar with their passions. Who is their favorite athlete? Music group? What is their favorite TV program? Etc. Remember what sounds like music to some teenagers may sound like a train wreck to you. *Be knowledgeable.* Try to show **_WITH-IT-NESS_**. I am not saying that you have to talk or dress like a teenager. The greatest compliment that a teen could give us is, **"YOU ARE REAL."** <u>Know where they are coming from.</u> Be all things to all people. When I first entered the educational field, I knew I would need to be in tune with their interests. I constantly watched MTV, (even though some of the music made me want to throw up) so that I could be aware of the music my students were listening to.

For example, one day while working as a high school guidance counselor, I stepped out of my office and noticed a young man leaning against the wall of our office hallway. He had very long hair, several earrings and was wearing a "Metallica" T-shirt. For those who are not familiar with Metallica, they are a speed \ heavy metal band. Recently, I had taken the time to watch MTV and viewed Metallica's newest music video, "And Justice For All."

I asked him if I could be of help. He informed me he was waiting to meet with my colleague. I then asked him if he had seen this particular music video. He looked at me and his eyes grew to the size of silver dollars. He said, "Mr. Petro, you know Metallica? You listen to Metallica? You like Metallica?" (You do know I could only honestly answer one of those questions.) I had connected. **I was in his world now.** Every time I would see John in the halls or throughout the school he would come to talk with me. A bond was formed. Teenagers want to know that someone does care for them and is interested in their **TOTAL** lives.

As I looked at the big picture, my small choice to recognize John's interests impacted his life. It probably took me no more then **10 seconds** to notice his shirt and make the statement I did. In reality, every time I watched MTV I was preparing myself for John type encounters.

> **"The will to win is important,
> but the will to <u>prepare</u> is vital."**
> *— Joe Paterno*

I remember another **10 second** encounter I had with a student. While sitting at my desk in my counseling office working on that dreaded paper work, I noticed Grigorios (Greg) Giannakopoulos, a senior at Great Bridge High School, passing by. Greg was the epitome of awesome students. He was the dream child \ student for every parent, teacher, coach, counselor, club sponsor, pastor, priest, rabbi, doctor, dentist, principal, brother, sister – you get the picture. Greg had a weighted GPA of almost 4.0 – he scored 1200 on his SAT – was a star foot ball player – involved in many school student activities \ clubs-involved in his church – volunteered in his community and even found time to work at a family owned restaurant.

I summoned Greg to come in my office and asked him about his college plans. He rambled off several very prestigious schools in Virginia. I then asked him if he had ever thought of the possibility of attending an Ivy league school, plus maybe having the opportunity of playing football there. Greg looked at me as if I had 10 heads and responded to me like I must be talking about someone else. (It wasn't the first time a student looked at me that way). This was Greg's senior year of high school and the first year he ever was allowed to play organized football. From my teaching and coaching experience I felt Greg had what it would take to be a student-athlete at a NCAA division I-AA program.

At the time of this writing, Greg has begun his second year of law school at the University of Richmond. I am proud to say, he graduated from Princeton University with a degree in Political science – after having the privilege of playing four years of college football, in which Princeton University won the Ivy league championship twice. How long did it take me to call Greg in my office and talk to him about an Ivy league school. **10 Seconds! In a matter of <u>10 seconds</u> Greg's life was changed forever.**

Young people will live up to the expectations set for them. When I experienced my tragedy, no one had to tell the 900 students of Santa Fe High school in Alta Loma, Texas to rally around me. No one had to tell them to pack out the church in the middle of a hurricane for my first wife Ava's funeral service. No one had to tell them to stand in pouring rain, with mud up to their knees at the cemetery, to let me know how much they loved me. They automatically responded. Why? Because they were sponges who had absorbed all the **10 second** moments of love that Coach Petrocelli had for each one of them. When it was time for them to be squeezed, the love they had absorbed came out. That's all they knew to do – to give back what had saturated their hearts.

Think of this: the heart, mind, body and spirit of young people (actually all people) are like sponges. Whatever it soaks up or takes in throughout life will be released when squeezed. As the expression goes: "Garbage in, Garbage out. Positive in, Positive out."

It is so rewarding to think that maybe one of my **10 second** decisions or actions has impacted someones life. Receiving letters, cards and phones calls from thankful students, parents, teachers and administrators is so gratifying. In my travels as a speaker I always wonder what type of difference I am making. The responses from so many reaffirm my calling.

Recently, a young high student approached me after an assembly. With tear filled eyes she explained how recently she tried to commit suicide. These were tears of joy. The reason, after hearing my presentation, she now understood how **10 seconds** would not only have taken her life but effected so many other lives. She was thankful to me for my message and would now tell others how **10 seconds could change lives forever**.

Young people need to understand the great benefits or great consequences that are associated with each decision they make. Whether they choose to make a good or bad **10 second decision**, they have <u>control</u> over their decisions. There can't be any excuses. They must own up to their choices. It's better for them not to wait for a crisis to discover what's important in life. Bigger isn't always better, and going faster is not necessarily progress. Encourage them to be content with what they have but not always who they are. There is always room for improvement. **Working at making better 10 second decisions is essential!**

Encourage children to be persistent in expressing their creativity with unconditional love. They can never be too busy to say "please" and "thank you." Many of the faults we have as adults, are exactly the ones our parents tried to correct when we were children. It only takes **10 seconds** to say "I love you" or "I am sorry" or "forgive me." To give a great big hug or a compliment is a **10 second** action. It is the simple things in life that matter. Life does not continue day by day. It continues second by second – **10 seconds** at a time. Seize every **10 second** decision, moment and action. We can all make a difference...**10 SECONDS AT A TIME!**

"I've learned that if you keep doing what you've always done, you'll keep getting what you've always gotten."
— *Unknown*

The Power of the Dream

by
SANDY QUEEN

The Power of
the Dream

by
SANDY QUEEN

Following a session with students in an alternative school, one young man turned to me and asked, *"Lady, when you go home after working with us, do you have to get a therapist to help you with all the problems you hear about?"* I was both amused and astounded by the question, because it hit at the heart of my experiences with young people over the last eighteen years. The young man next to him asked the question, *"When are you gonna write the book?"* Perhaps this chapter is a beginning to that end.

Many times, I am invited to a school as part of Safe and Drug Free School funding. Want to know the first thing I tell kids from the platform? *"We don't have a drug problem in this country!"* We don't. We don't have a drug problem. We don't have an alcohol problem. We don't have a problem with teens and sex. We don't even have a problem with violence, dropouts, or gangs. We have a NEED problem.

When I looked at the students in that alternative school that day, I saw a microcosm of the young people I have seen throughout my travels; students who are having trouble making it (not to be confused with being a "trouble maker"). Troublemakers ARE the problem; kids who are having trouble making it HAVE a problem. One seems hopeless; the other has hope. This particular group included young people from a myriad of backgrounds, but to a student, they had one thing in common; a need – many times unrealized; a need – many times unspoken, but a need that found its way to the surface through the attitudes and behaviors that had earned them an "invitation" to this classroom setting.

When kids are little, they accept what goes on in their families as "normal." Even if it is unpleasant or scary, they often don't realize there are other ways of being. That's why many children accept abuse as a normal part of life. That's why many of us learned coping skills as children to help us survive, that as adults, away from those early beginnings, no longer have survival value for us. Yet, many of us continue to hang on to them even though they are a detriment to our mental and emotional well-being, not to mention the stability of our relationships and families. These coping skills may include such behaviors as withdrawal, codependency, hyper-vigilance, overachieving, pleasing...the list goes on and on!

As young people reach what developmental psychologist Piaget termed the "formal operational stage" when they can engage in deductive reasoning, they often realize that they have missed out on some basic things, like caring and validation and love. This comes at a time when their greatest personal psychological issue is forming a stable identity for themselves. The need to belong is powerful. This is not wrong or abnormal. The peer group is the strongest force in the adolescent's life, even for kids from "good families." The clothes, the hair, the jewelry – all relatively harmless symbols of identity with the peer group. Unfortunately, for many teens, the need to be "someone" goes beyond these superficial symbols to the darker side of sex and drugs and violence. For teens from families who have not been able to provide the love and encouragement needed for healthy transitioning, this can be a time of turmoil.

A teenager's biggest need is warm responsiveness and caring from their parents. In spite of their protests to the contrary, teens need to know that those who are supposed to care for them do, in fact, care for them. This doesn't mean they will be appreciative for the caring! They're not ready to do that – yet. This takes a few more years and the realizations that the electric company really does turn off the power when you don't pay the bill, and food doesn't miraculously appear in the refrigerator! It takes moving away from home and getting some perspective on what we have tried to help them learn. Young people who haven't had this guidance are often angry and lonely and turn to sex and drugs, not for the "highs" but for the momentary relief from the hurt and anger.

When presenting to high school audiences, I often make this statement: *"Gentlemen, there is at least one of you in this room right now that would give ANYTHING if your dad would walk through that door and walk up here and stand beside me and look out at you and say, 'Son, I love you. I'm so proud to be your dad. I'm so proud to have you as my son.'"* I don't have to ask which young men in that auditorium are lacking that man in their lives. They tell me by acting out or making fun of me, or talking, or laughing... doing anything to avoid having to deal with the feelings. The fact is, many of them will never hear that from their fathers because they can't, or won't, say it. The fact is, some of the boys wouldn't recognize their own father if he walked in because they have never met. That's not condemnation; it's reality.

To the girls I say, *"Ladies, we often go looking for love in all the wrong places."* The stories I have heard from young people over the years would fill a book, but they all have the same underlying theme: <u>need</u>. The need for adults in their lives to validate their lives with love and caring; the need to feel they have worth; the need to belong to something or someone who cares.

One young man in a high school near Toronto, Canada, left the auditorium during an assembly. He returned after the assembly to speak with me and he began to cry. This was a big kid, star athlete, popular. He had <u>everything</u> going for him.

"You know," he began, *"I'm the star athlete here. I play three sports and I play them all well. I've been playing since I was six years old. Want to know why? So my dad would be proud of me. Want to know how many games my dad has seen me play? Not one, ever! My mom is great. She takes me to all the tournaments. She's there for me. I've already signed on to play professional hockey. I don't have to wonder what I'm going to do with my life. But I tell you,"* he added amid his tears, *"I would give it all up right now, ALL of it, if that man would walk in that door and stand up here next to you and look at me and tell me he loves me. Want to know how many girls I've been to bed with? About thirty-five or forty. And you want to know why? Because it's the only way I have to prove to myself that I'm a man. No one has ever shown me another way."*

Need.

A sixteen year-old girl shared her story with me after her high school assembly. *"I've had unprotected intercourse with every boy I've known since I was nine years old,"* she explained, *"and the reason is exactly what you said up there; no one has ever said they cared about me except during sex. I know they don't mean it. I'm smart enough to figure that out, but at least for those few minutes I hear what I never hear any other time."*

I asked her what she would do if she became pregnant. Her answer was the same as I have received from probably 90% of the teen girls I have posed that question to in the last eighteen years, *"At least I'd have someone to love me...."*

Need.

A ninth grader sat with me behind the curtain on the school stage because he didn't want anyone to see him cry. He was the school "tough kid" and he took a real risk in sharing his feelings with me. *"I'd give anything to hear those words from my dad,"* he began, *"but you're right. I wouldn't know the man if he walked in here because I've never met him. But I would settle for hearing them from my mom. But she's either drunk, asleep, with her boyfriend, or yelling at me when I get home from school. So I drop my books off, go to my buddy's house and we smoke pot for three hours every night. I get completely stoned. I come home, exhausted, drop into bed, get up the next day and do it all over again."*

What should we say to him at this point? We could remind him that marijuana is illegal and getting caught with it could land him in jail. He doesn't care. *"At least when I'm stoned,"* he said, *"I don't feel the pain."*

We could appeal to his intellect. *"You know, this is the ninth grade. This is the year your grades really begin to count. You really ought to focus on those grades if you want to get out of high school and into college."*

He doesn't care. Like a lot of teens, it's difficult for him to look beyond what is happening now. It's hard to study when you hurt. So, how do we reach this young man and the others like him who are hurting? What do we say that can make any sense at all to them?

The question I asked him is the only one, I believe, that makes sense. It's the only one that each of us can answer at whatever stage we happen to find ourselves. It is one that only each of us can answer for ourselves.

"What is your dream?" I asked him. *"What do you want to have happen when your mother is no longer an issue, when every day belongs only to you to do with as you please. What do you want to have happen?"*

Without hesitation, he replied, *"I want to be a pilot. I want to fly."*

Even in very serious moments, we can share some lightness. This was one of those moments. *"You can't fly when you're already high,"* I reminded him. *"You have to come down first! I fly three of four days out of every week and I don't want the pilot sitting up there in that cockpit at 35,000 feet stoned out of his mind. I want him stone cold sober!"* He then smiled.

"However, that is a wonderful dream." I continued. *"There's your dream. Here's your reality. There are two things you're going to have to have do to make your dream come true. First, you need to graduate from high school. Second, you need to be drug free because they will test you. The question is not can you stop using drugs and get passing grades. The question is: do you have what it takes to make your dream come true?"*

"I think I do," he replied.

"Good," I said. *"I'll be back tomorrow with someone I think can help you. I can't be here every day, and you need someone here to help you on a daily basis."*

"I'm going home tonight and I'm not going to smoke any pot," he declared. *"I want you to know that I can do this."*

"I'm not asking you to do this for me," I reminded him. *"I'm asking you to focus on your dream because, you see, you will find a way to do what is important to you."*

The next day I returned with a friend of mine who is a marvelous counselor for teens in need. Our young man met us, rather dejected. *"I didn't make it last night,"* he said quietly, *"but I smoked for two hours instead of three."*

What do we say to him at this point? *"You've got a long way to go,"* or, *"Way to go"*? When I congratulated him on his success, he was surprised. *"You mean, I did something good?"*

"Let me put it to you this way," I said, *"If I gave you $100 today and you brought me 33% interest tomorrow, I'd find a lot of money to invest with you because you are a great risk. You're on your way to your dream."*

What do we need to do to help our young people deal with their needs? How do we help them realize their dreams? Here are some things we can do:

1. Stop dealing with the "symptom" and begin dealing with the "disease." Drugs, sex, truancy, gangs, are all symptoms of deeper issues. If I had a headache, you might offer me an aspirin. However, you don't know WHY I have that headache. I could be hungry or tired. I could have been out in the sun too long, or even have a brain tumor! To offer me an aspirin as a panacea for my headache is much like offering the "programs" for drug prevention. They may relieve the symptom, but the problem may remain.

2. Treat all young people with warm positive regard, even the difficult ones.

3. Stop seeing "troublemakers" and begin to see "kids who are having trouble making It." There is a vast difference.

4. Give them sense of hope by believing in them even when they don't believe in themselves.

5. Help them realize short-term dreams. If they can make a five-minute dream come true, they can work on longer ones. We're not asking kids to see into the future, but to work on what is important to them.

The answer to the question from that young man mentioned in the beginning of this article: Yes. Sometimes I DO need some help in processing some of the painful stories I hear during my work. But there are so many instances when the few minutes we do spend together seem to help these kids get at least a glimmer of a new perspective.

A sixteen-year-old girl wanted to take her own life because she had been abandoned by both parents and mostly ignored by the great grandparent with whom she lived. We talked for a long time one day, exploring options. I told her she could die any time, but we only get once chance at this living thing. I encouraged her to spend the next two years learning to live; friends, school, activities, and THEN decide about her life. She saw no way to get to college, even though her grades were good. The guidance staff at her school helped determine that her biggest risk was just saying, *"I need."* Several months after our meeting at one of our peer mediation training sessions, a delightful young woman showed up with a great new attitude and a desire to help other young people. Her message to that group of young people that day was, *"Don't take lightly what we are doing here today. Sometimes all it takes is for one person to let you know they care to turn your life around. Maybe you could be that one person for someone else. I dream of helping other kids find that someone cares."*

The power of the dream.

The "Why" Factor – *How to Keep Teens on Your Team!*

by
ERIC CHESTER

The "Why" Factor –
How to Keep Teens on Your Team!

by
ERIC CHESTER

S andy was fervently cleaning a patient's teeth who obviously hadn't flossed since Ol' Blue was a pup. I knew this to be painfully true because the teeth her tools were refurbishing were inside <u>my</u> mouth. Doc Sweeney had reminded me during each of my semi-annual visits to adopt the habit of flossing. But I had never really been shown how and thought that a good brushing twice a day (with plenty of elbow grease applied to the brush) would more than suffice. Besides, I'm a busy guy! Who's got time for such a minor detail?

As time slowly passed, I grew anxious. With each stroke of her oral weaponry, I tried to figure out what I had done to make this young white-coated whippersnapper want to hurt me so badly. This was supposed to be a routine cleaning, not a torture session. Let me tell you – I was in pure agony!

When the sandblasting finally ended, Sandy laid down her heavy artillery and began a ten-minute lecture I won't ever forget. *"Eric, you are a good brusher. Your teeth are very white. But I'd like to show you how we can avoid what you just went through and actually look forward to our next encounter."* Then, using a replica model of a mouth and some floss, she proceeded to give me a life-changing demonstration. I learned that gums are like a layer of carpet where termite-like food bacteria can hide from even the best toothbrush. *"This bacteria clings to the roots of the teeth. Those roots are like pylons which anchor your teeth to the foundation of your jaw."* She continued, *"In time, bacteria can destroy those pylons and your teeth will become brittle and fall out."* Then she went a step further. She took out the floss and showed me how to lace it through my fingers. She demonstrated how to scrape away the "pesky termites" which had made a comfortable home in my mouth. *"The termites will try to return every time you eat, Eric. So it is your challenge to use floss to scrape your pylons at least once a day so your teeth remain in your head."* Her final words said it all. *"The next time we get together, I'd like to think that we can get you on your way in a matter of minutes with no discomfort and a healthier smile on your face. But that's entirely up to you! Happy flossing!"*

At that moment, at age 38, I had been taught a lesson by a 24-year-old hygienist that would forever change how each of my coming days would begin. Instead of merely being **told** to floss (which my mother and dentist had done *so* many times before), I had finally learned **why**.

As a parent or an educator (or both), you're responsible for *telling* teens what to do. You probably give a lot of orders. I know I do. *"Make your bed." "Don't hit your brother!" "Sit up straight." "Do your homework." "Eat your spinach." "Don't you look at me in that tone of voice!"* Do any of these phrases sound familiar? We should give orders, right? After all, we know more than they do, and our parents and teachers told us what to do! And we did it, by God, because if we didn't, we'd get "you know what" by "you know who!"

This much I know. **Teens of this new generation are different.** Although some follow orders, most question authority and rebel against conformity like never before. Granted, some are more aggressive than others in their approach. Yet the underlying belief system is universal: today's teens *demand* to be treated "fairly" and handled with respect. They *expect* "privileges" and have an inflated sense of their "rights." And they do not conform to rules merely because there are rules in place. They must know why.

If you are connected to this generation (because you're reading this book I'm assuming you are), I am only putting into words what you already know to be true. So what are your options? Yell louder than they do? Pray for the day when they leave home? Drop back and punt?

The answers may be easier than most of us think. I believe the way to keep teens "tuned in" and "turned on" to family, school, and life is simple: <u>Give them what they want</u>. And what they want is the *why*.

One thing that has been handed down through generations is the "Kid Code." It still goes like this:

"The only things which matter to me are those things which matter to me, so if what you're saying doesn't matter to me, then it simply does not matter to me!"

No, not everything *mattered to us* as a kid. No, we didn't do everything we were told. But we complied with most of what was asked of us and did most of what we were told to do. That's just the way it used to be. But as the 60's rock 'n' roll legend Bob Dylan sings, *"These times, they are a changin'."*

This generation *demands* "value." They *demand* to know the <u>why</u> behind the <u>what</u>. Sure, when we were young and our parents were young, we *wanted* value by having the <u>why</u> spelled out for us. We just didn't *demand* it so loudly, nor did we *rebel* so visibly when our questions weren't answered.

Stated simply, today's teens want things to have *immediate relevance* in their lives. That is our challenge. To make what we want them to think, know, learn, and do *matter* to them. If we build value (the why) behind the concept (the what), this generation will amaze you with their determination to succeed and their ingenuity (the how) in finding solutions.

Sounds great in theory, but does this work in practice? Absolutely! Here's a three-tier strategy proven effective in modern day adolescent motivation and performance.

First, Know "Their" World

The foundation of success for any great salesperson is knowing their customer inside and out. The sales pro must take the time to learn and understand the hopes and the dreams of each prospect. Then, and only then, can they tie a product or service into the customers' world and show "them" how it solves "their" problems and/or makes "their" dreams come true. The focus is, of course, on "them."

Like the superstars in sales, we need to know our customers (the kids) inside and out. This is best achieved through in-depth conversation and consistent casual observation. Your research can begin by diving head-first into life as "they" know it.

From time to time (or as much as you can stand it) watch their movies and listen to their music. Ask open-ended questions and let them give their opinions openly, without fear of being told they are wrong. For example, you could ask, *"What did you think about the election?"* or *"Who do you think is the best _____ of all time?"* Take careful note of their role models and interests. Keep totally abreast of current teen fashions, trends, and slang. Walk through an arcade or drop in on a high school dance. Watch an hour of MTV and ESPN-2 per week and check out the advertisements targeting young people through all forms of media.

CAUTION: Brace yourself. What you discover may alarm you. But wouldn't you rather know what you're up against and be prepared to deal with it, than be caught off-guard and find yourself "shell-shocked"?

Knowing "their" world also means knowing how they assimilate information. I often ask teachers how current they are with respect to the subject they are teaching and how recent trends, developments, and technological breakthroughs have impacted their respective areas of expertise. I also challenge them to look deeply at their methods of sharing their knowledge with students. If we are going to stand any chance of holding the attention of a teen who is growing up in the age of a 500-channel television, laser disc learning, and the internet, we need to know more than they know <u>and</u> present it in a way that keeps them captivated. Research has shown that young viewers give a television advertisement a total of three seconds to grab their attention or it will get "zapped" by the remote control. *Are you getting zapped?*

Secondly, Know Your Message

With each interaction with a teenager, we need to ask ourselves if there is lesson or a point we are trying to impart. If the answer is "yes," we should have a clear idea of <u>what</u> it is and <u>why</u> it is important to them. *"Because I said so,"* and *"Just do as you're told"* have gone the way of leisure suits, Mr. T, and the Cabbage Patch Doll. Even though this outdated command giving style may stir action, the result is only temporary.

Often times we teach kids the same stuff we were taught because, well...because it is something we were taught. However, as "authority figures," we are given an unspecified and limited supply of bullets from which to use in our guns. Why should you use up your precious ammo on unimportant concepts and lessons? If the point being made is not relevant or necessary, don't fire your gun! I'd rather ask my kids (and I have four between the ages of 12 and 17) to do one thing that is relevant and necessary, than to ask them to do ten things and hope they will take action on the one that is actually important. When I make only one request, they understand its importance and act accordingly

The way I see it, if you harp on kids everyday about taking out the trash and eating lima beans, maybe they will have turned you off when you talk to them about getting into a car with a friend who has had too much to drink or letting a date get out of hand. Knowing our message means that we know our true mission and have a clear vision of what we <u>really</u> want our kids to take into the world.

Knowing our message also encompasses knowing ourselves and what <u>we</u> are all about. (Here's where some of my audiences start to squirm.) To be effective with today's teens, we must remain consistent with our message and "walk our talk." Many of us remember the old *"do as I say, not as I do"* standard from our childhood. Again, this principle no longer holds water. It's tough to lecture a kid about driving too fast when they see a radar detector on our dashboard. It is difficult to keep a teen honest and open with us if they've just overheard our phone conversation where we told a fib to get out of a meeting. If we don't "practice what we preach," this generation will eat us for breakfast. There needs to be clearly-defined reasons for what we do and do not do. Our decisions must be in alignment with our personal values. We must never forget that what we are modeling with our lives speaks so loudly that it drowns out what we are saying.

Lastly, "Connect The Dots"

A football team can have a talented quarterback and a sensational receiver but still have difficulty completing a pass. However, a good coach knows the dynamics of both elements in the relationship and is therefore able to help make a connection. TRANSLATION: You may know "their" world and you may know "your" stuff, but if you don't make a solid connection between the two, the end result will be an incomplete pass.

Here's how the principal of a small middle school "connected the dots" to solve a problem with a few of his older female students who were wearing lipstick. After applying it, they would press their lips to the bathroom mirror and leave lip prints. He needed a creative way to put an end to it and did the following.

He gathered all the girls together that wore lipstick and brought them to the girls' bathroom after school. He explained that it was becoming a problem for the custodian (who was standing nearby) to clean the mirror every night. He said he felt the ladies did not fully understand just how much of a problem it was and wanted them to witness just how hard it was to clean. The custodian then demonstrated by taking a long, bristly brush out of a box. He then dipped the brush in the nearest toilet (yuck!) moved to the mirror and proceeded to scrub away the lipstick. That was the last day the girls pressed their lips on the mirror. This demonstration helped "connect the dots" for the girls, and they had a sufficient reason (the why) to stop.

Consider the following underlying questions throughout your relationship(s) with teens:

1. How does what you want them to think (or know/ learn/do) benefit them? NOTE: A benefit can also be the avoidance of a negative result, as illustrated above.

2. How can this benefit (value to them) be emphasized so that the message (concept) will be understood and internalized?

This is what "connecting the dots" is all about. Making stuff matter. Finding the relevance and emphasizing it in our communication with young people.

For me, nothing works better than a good analogy. As one who is routinely placed in front of thousands of teens with the responsibility of "motivating" them, I am always loaded with entertaining analogies to help make my points. By painting visual pictures with my words and gestures, I am able to illustrate concepts teens may not be familiar with and reinforce those they may know, but haven't fully comprehended.

Already in this chapter, I've employed several analogies to help me connect with you (e.g. the dental hygienist, salesperson, bullets in your guns, football coach). Hopefully, I have touched on issues which you find relevant and shown that I know a little about your world and the challenges you are facing with the teen(s) in your life. Further, I trust that I have demonstrated that I know my message and I am congruent with my beliefs. My primary tool (pardon the analogy) for bridging the gap between my message and your world is the analogy. I learned from the best.

My dad has always been one of the world's great storytellers. Often times around the dinner table, he'd launch some incredibly long dissertation about something out of the blue, leaving my sisters and I staring at each other in bewilderment, wondering (but never, ever vocalizing),

"Where in tarnation is he going with this one?" But our questions never went unanswered, as each story always carried a strong message that somehow connected with each of us on a different level, getting through the walls of rebellion we had erected, stimulating both thought and action.

Grant Chester knew his kids, his message, *and why it was important.* He was a master at connecting the dots. With only a 10th grade education, but a Ph.D. in life, my father used the power of the analogy with the precision of a surgeon to penetrate young hearts and minds.

My hope is that you will use this three-tier strategy to empower the teens in your sphere of influence. Understand their world, know your message, and connect the dots. By giving them the "why" they've come to expect, we can expect great things from teens of this generation.

Funhouse or Madhouse?
Becoming Love's Reflection

by
JOHN CRUDELE

TEEN
POWER

Funhouse or Madhouse?
Becoming Love's Reflection

by
J OHN C RUDELE

A s a child, I couldn't wait to go to the carnival when it came to town. I found one of the wildest experiences in the house of mirrors. Those curvy mirrors made me look so distorted and silly – tall, short, fat, thin. What a laugh! Then, within minutes I'd be back out in the sunlight and reality. Imagine if you grew up in that house of mirrors. It would become your reality, and you would believe that was the way you really looked. Kind of scary. Well...families form a house of mirrors with either straight or curvy mirrors, depending on the health and availability of the parents. Teams, classes, churches and society form another house of mirrors.

Children become what they see in these mirrors. At an early age they develop a sense of identity through those who choose to love and to not love them, from what others say and don't say and from what others do and don't do. Relationships within the family unit, the classroom and their peer-group or community sharpen those impressions.

Our identity always exists in relationship to someone or something else. We look at the earth in relation to the sun and the moon in relation to the earth. The moon is not a moon by itself. It is a moon because it circles the earth. Its *relation* to earth gives the moon its unique identity. If it floated freely in space it would be something else. A man becomes a husband based on his *relationship* with his wife. Through bearing a child, a woman becomes a mother and the husband a father. Naturally, kids discover their identity in their relationship with their moms and dads. Whether those relationships are healthy and supportive or insecure and fragmented, directly affects a child. As author John Powell, S.J. says, "We are the product of those who have loved us...or refused to love us. Whoever we are called to love or is supposed to love us has power over forming our identity...whether they love us or not!"

Reflecting Availability

When I was a swimmer at Ames High School in Iowa, Coach Wittmer expected the whole team to stay after school for about two hours. In my rebelliousness I'd exclaim, "that's ridiculous, coach. I think if you could give us a 1000 yard, quality-time workout, we could be out of here in about 15 minutes." Coach insisted, "Good things just take time...Now get in the pool!"

To consistently succeed in showing your child how much you love him or her, consider the amount of time you spend in their life. Being available teaches them that they are valuable and important. Moreover, consistent availability gives parents ample opportunity to meet their child's natural desire for affection, instruction and role modeling. To get enough of that nurturing, kids need their parents' time – and the more the better. Still, over the past 20 or 30 years, our time-crunched society created the notion of "quality time."

Have you heard about quality time? "Hey, we don't have much time, but the time we have is 'quality time.'" As life gets busier, however, "quality time" is being substituted for "any time." So, often instead of *rebuilding* the family, parents *redefine* and *restructure* the family with "quality time." Quality time or not, some spend only minutes per day with their children. Compare that to past generations. Then, parents spent two to three hours per day interacting in a meaningful way with their kids. Now, fathers average two minutes a day in one-on-one conversation with each child, while mothers double that time to about four minutes a day. That's only 15 to 30 minutes a week!

Children clearly sense love when they're invited to share what's important to them. They spell love T-I-M-E and, for better or for worse, time and power go hand in hand. It's not peer pressure prompting their decisions now and later. It's only peer influence. Whoever spends time with your children has power over them. Typically, children talk one-on-one with their friends for two to three hours a day. Ask yourself, "What can I do to increase our time together?" Have you really listened to your children and defined time through their needs, rather than by your convenient availability? As Coach said, "Good things just take time."

Reflecting Acceptance and Appreciation

With increased parental availability, kids naturally pull mom and dad into better focus. Of course, children discover themselves in what their parents project on them as well. Remember the Rudolf the Red Nose Reindeer story? He came into the world not knowing that he was different until his mom, dad, other reindeer and Santa pointed it out. Until his parents and community treated him as a misfit, he didn't feel like one. Rudolf's coach shouted, "We're not going to let Rudolf play in any Reindeer games." His dad even tried covering Rudolf's nose, sending the clear message: "There is something wrong with you." Do you see Rudolf's dilemma? Rudolf wasn't *accepted*, and therefore, he felt *insecure*. Now vulnerable, Rudolf found an unconditional source of acceptance and love in his girlfriend, Clarise. Rudolf even joined a gang! Cornelius, the eldest misfit, gained the power of surrogate parent and gang leader! Together, they went off to help the misfit toys, pull some teeth, guide a sleigh and save Christmas. They did all this, just to discover their value.

Like Rudolf, people feel insecure when shown performance-based love. Those individuals believe they must do something to gain acceptance, and they become "human doings" instead of "human beings." Knowing this, parents can reflect a clear image to their kids by consistently showing concern and love without strings attached. Security results. "You cleaned the dishes...thank you" or "you earned an A...I'm proud or you" sends a healthier message than "I love you when you do the dishes or receive good grades." *Grade the paper; love and accept the person.*

Besides genuinely accepting someone, appreciate them. How? Catch them doing something right. When accepted, children feel secure. When appreciated for their contribution, children feel significant. Let's receive our children first...and then respond.

Reflecting Affection

Ideally, intimacy between parents and their children adjusts mirrors in the house and reveals a more real representation of each individual. In Margery Williams' story, *The Velveteen Rabbit,* the characters cherish being "real." At one point, Rabbit asks Skin Horse, "What is REAL? Does it mean having things that buzz inside you and a stick-out handle?"

Skin Horse explains that real has less to do with how you're made and more to do with how you're treated. Smiling he points out, "Real is something that happens to you when a child chooses to love you for a long, long period of time. It doesn't happen all at once, or for people who break easily, or have sharp edges, or who have to be carefully kept."

Everyone becomes more "real" when loved. Not surprisingly, the three most powerful words a child can hear are **"I love you."** How often do you say it? How often do they hear it? A wife once said to her husband, "I can't tell if you love me." The husband retorted, "I told you I loved you when I married you. If that ever changes, I'll let you know." Regardless of his reasoning, she apparently needed to hear "I love you" more often and so does your child.

Affectionate touch communicates love as well. It needs to be safe, however, and needs to be a "giving" touch versus a "taking" touch. Unfortunately, the absence of parental affection creates a void or a vacuum that a child may strive to fill elsewhere. Lacking physical contact, many young people starve from "skin thirst" or "touch deficit" and may use sexual touch as a substitute. As a parent, you reduce your child's risk of this by being available and affectionate. In this way, moms and dads reinforce their message of love and bless their sons and daughters.

The words **"I want you,"** along with the corresponding actions, make a tremendous connection with a child. Many children hear that they are loved; they're just not sure if they're wanted. I met Jonathan on the set of the Ricki Lake Show. When it was his turn to speak into the camera, he said he wished his mother would have had an abortion rather than having him when she did. He went on to say, "I wish my mother would have waited to have me."

In my segment I exclaimed to Jonathan, "Your mother couldn't wait to have you, if she would have, you would have been your sister! Though you may have been conceived in a mistake, there are no mistakes. You're a miracle Jonathan!" Jonathan needs to sense that he is wanted and is a gift!

Then there is **"I need you!"** Young people and adults often become needy to the degree that they were not needed as children. "I can't break-up. My boyfriend needs me! I can't give up my child up for adoption. She needs me!" This young woman believes she's lovable because her boyfriend and baby needs her. Yet, this unhealthy need to be needed paralyzes her maturation. It's really she that needs the boyfriend and baby and, in her insecurity, she's not willing to let go. Stephen Glen, author of *Developing Capable Young People* shares, "It's not what we do for our children that helps them feel capable, but rather what we allow and invite them to do for and with us that helps them feel like a valuable person." Invite your children to contribute and feel needed by your family, class or team. This fosters their sense of security.

Finally, children crave hearing **"I believe in you."** Being believed in energizes a child to do their best and, when hurting, to hang on and not compromise. Belief sustains courage and hope.

Heart-felt phrases like "I love you," "I want you," "I need you" and "I believe in you" help children realize their value and purpose, and have a sense of security and hope. Not surprisingly, this type of interaction transforms the way a child functions both in and outside the family.

Reflecting Accountability and Authority

Besides reflecting words and actions to help your child mature, invite and allow for natural consequences when they fail to be accountable to their responsibilities. Consequences need to be predictable and agreed upon in advance as logical and fair. The key lesson? Explain that the privileges of life usually hinge on demonstrating responsibility. By giving up responsibility, by choosing not to follow previously agreed upon and clearly understood expectations, the child foregoes privileges. For example, sometimes students say, "The teacher gave me an 'F.'" No, the teacher didn't. The student worked all semester to earn that "F."

When parents inconsistently discipline, their children actually lose respect for them. For instance, when parents teach their kids about integrity and responsibility, and then put fuzz busters in their cars, they model this message: "If I speed and I don't get caught, I'm being responsible. If I speed and I do get caught, I'm being irresponsible." The child interprets the message, "Okay, if I drink alcohol and I don't get caught, I'm responsible. If I drink and get caught, I'm irresponsible." Is the message about right and wrong or about not getting caught? Ask yourself, "Am I reinforcing, justifying and rationalizing self-defined values or reflecting the truth for my children?" Teaching your children what to value, through your words and example, sends a message of love.

This approach challenges even the most well-meaning parents. Imagine, for instance, that the guys' football or girls' basketball team makes it all the way to the finals. After winning the district competition, you discover that some of the starters, including your son or daughter, make the mistake of consuming alcohol at a party. Do you call the school knowing the principal will suspend your child from athletics for several weeks and the final competitions? Whew! This is called "tough love" and it wins few popularity contests. Your children need parents, teachers and coaches that love them enough to take a stand against irresponsible behavior. Such adults are thinking long term, not just over next two weeks.

No matter their maturity level, our culture frequently empowers children to be their own ultimate authority at a very young age. But before developing a healthy sense of right and wrong, children need to admire and respect that character trait in someone else. We become what we admire – good or bad – so back to the house-of-mirrors. That's why positive exposure to parents, teachers, elders and God is so vital. International speaker and best selling author, Josh McDowell says, "Rules without relationships, leads to rebellion." I believe rules with relationships, lead to respect. Focus on creating loving relationships with consistent discipline, and respect will follow.

Final Reflections

According to psychiatrist Dr. Rudolf Dreikurs, misbehavior is "a mistaken interpretation on how to achieve significance and belonging." Misbehavior often signals a child's discouragement and/or their unmet need for love and connectedness. Quite possibly neither they, nor their parents, even know what is missing.

The fear of failure seems to shape some classic attitudes surrounding misbehavior. As hope, purpose and a sense of worth diminish for boys, for example, they tend to reject authority. Girls, on the other hand, tend to reject themselves. Note that each of the following points insulates a person from failure. Does your child exhibit any of the following attitudes? Here may be some reasons why.

- **I don't care.** *Because if I care and fail, I'm a failure. But if I don't care and fail, I didn't really fail.*

- **Afraid to try.** *If I try and fail, I'm a failure. But if I don't try and fail, I successfully failed by not trying. So in a strange way I didn't really fail.*

- **Won't play the game.** *If I play the game and fail, then I failed. But if I'm not in the game, I can't fail. I then nurture and sustain these attitudes by joining a group where it is cool not to care, to try or to play the game.*

In situations like these, try acknowledging "effort" before "success." This illuminates and validates in the child what they are able to control.

Beliefs, feelings, and thoughts drive all behaviors. Effective parenting, teaching and coaching becomes an exercise in understanding a child's behavior through a better understanding of their point of reference. Then parents can effectively bridge children from where they are, to where they need to be, while loving them unconditionally each and every step along the way.

What life-messages are your children receiving? Glance in the mirror. Who do you see? Who do you think your child sees? Some of the attitudes and actions parents and children mirror to one another may need adjusting for a healthier perspective. Each day, forgive and begin again. Whatever the distortions, clarity begins with taking a second look at love's reflection.

Chalk One Up
For Laughter

by
SCOTT FRIEDMAN

Chalk One Up
For Laughter
by
SCOTT FRIEDMAN

I f you're a victim of "teacher burnout" (and your students are arsonists), it's time to fight fire with fire. Pull the ultimate flame-thrower from your arsenal of tools – *humor*.

By using humor, you touch not only your students' minds, but their hearts and funny bones as well. As you move from merely informing to inspiring and entertaining, your students will pay closer attention to you and learn more in the process. Research has shown that humor in the classroom:

1. **Creates a positive learning environment**. Laughter is a sign that students are *enjoying* the learning instead of accepting it as a dull effort demanded of them by the teacher. Once you've shown that laughter is acceptable, the effect will be less anxiety and a positive reinforcing effect on each member of your class. This increases individual and group productivity, creativity, class discussion, and idea generation. In other words, it loosens up the mental gears.

2. **Influences students' relationship with the teacher.** When surveyed about what makes a good teacher, students consistently say that good teachers (in addition to knowing the subject) make the material interesting. Other studies show that humor is positively related to teacher competency evaluations and 93% of students view humor as an essential ingredient in teaching. Why? Humor forms a partnership. When you laugh with your students, you are inviting them into a relationship with you. When people laugh together, they forget their differences and share in the common experience laughter allows.

3. **Increases students' participation in the learning process.** Learners benefit from humor in several ways. When students can relate what they've learned to a memorable event, they are more likely to remember the information. Humor also increases attentiveness, interest, motivation to learn, and satisfaction with learning. It creates playfulness and a positive attitude. Humor also decreases academic stress, anxiety toward the subject matter, and class monotony. While you may think Calculus 101 is the hottest thing going, your students may find it quite dull. Humor is one way to bridge the gap and interest them in learning.

Education "superstars" understand these benefits and use humor to their advantage. Humor is a well-known strategy employed by Roberta Ford, who won *USA Today's* prestigious Teacher of the Year award in the late 1980's.

When asked about the most important qualities of a good teacher, Ms. Ford responded, "The two qualities are caring about kids and being both willing and able to engage them in learning. We used to meet students halfway. But we have so many students now who either can't or won't come halfway. It takes the teacher who is willing to go all the way to reach that child." Humor engages students in learning. It serves as the hook that reels them in and invites them to participate in the process.

One of my seminar participants confirmed this awesome power of humor. She worried about her son Brian because he didn't seem to fit in at school. Often he came home from school crying because the other kids didn't like him. One day, Brian raced home and proudly proclaimed that he had found the secret to making friends. "Just make them laugh," he beamed, "and they will like you." Now that you know the secret, how do you implement it?

How To Incorporate Humor In The Classroom

Humor is a skill that you can learn, develop, and internalize. I would guess that humorous thoughts often go through your mind, but you're afraid to say anything lest you appear foolish. Most people are naturally funny, but we're out of practice being ourselves! So take some risks and don't be too vested in the outcome. Have fun with it! To get you started, here are five techniques to add humor in your classroom.

1. Use Humor Aikido.

Aikido is a martial art in which the fighter blends with an oncoming force instead of opposing it. The fighter does not resist the opponent but rather uses and redirects the opponent's momentum.

For example, I was on a plane ride recently where someone kept mistakenly hitting the attendant call button when trying to adjust the volume on his headset. The flight attendant came over the intercom and said in an annoyed tone, "Will the person who is hitting the call button please stop!" By opposing the force, she created embarrassment and resentment in the passenger. She could have used the Aikido approach and said, "It appears that in an attempt to adjust the volume on your headset, someone is touching the flight attendant call button. If this continues, I'm sorry, but I'll have to ask you to go outside and play. Or you'll have to spend the rest of the flight with your seat belt on and your seat in its full upright and most uncomfortable position." Aikido involves reacting differently to the stressors in your life without reverting to old behavior patterns.

You can use Aikido with students to create open communication and cooperation. When they come out swinging, don't return the punch. Let's say a student screams at you, "You're too old to understand!" Your blood begins to boil and your reaction may be to lash back. Instead, pause, and look for the Aikido approach. You could say, "I'm as young as I can be for my age. Why don't you give me a chance?" An unexpected, positive response cushions the anger and redirects it without putting the student down.

Before using this technique, always ask yourself, "Where am I coming from?" If you're feeling hostile toward the student, your humor will reflect your feelings. Humor always mirrors the truth. Humor that reflects anger or bitterness may come out as sarcasm or a joke with a biting, caustic edge. If you're really angry, your safest bet is to poke fun at yourself instead of the student.

2. Use Self-Effacing Humor.

Charles Schultz, the creator of the *Peanuts* comic strip says, "Laughter is not just a pleasure – it's a necessity. It has long been my belief that one of the things that has enabled men and women to survive is the ability to laugh. If I were given the opportunity to present a gift to the next generation, it would be the ability for each individual to learn to laugh at themselves."

The ability to laugh at yourself and your own appearance, flaws, and foolishness is the ultimate achievement in humor. Laughing at yourself is acceptable when you do it with affection and tolerance toward yourself (i.e., you know you are flawed and silly, yet lovable). Your ability to laugh at yourself will make you appear more genuine, approachable, and human.

Self-effacing humor effectively defuses hostility. When you have an unfriendly encounter with a student, he or she expects you to fight back. If you make a self-effacing remark about yourself in a good-natured way, you throw the student off-balance. The student's options are to stay mad and fight (with no one fighting back) or laugh with you. Because you deflected the anger back on yourself, the student can rethink the situation and settle things peacefully without losing face.

Self-effacing humor can also help create a positive learning environment. If teachers make mistakes and can laugh at themselves, students discover that it's acceptable to make mistakes and learn from them. They feel more willing and able to share without anxiety. Teachers and parents who can "take" a joke teach their students to be equally flexible, forgiving, and tolerant.

3. Be More Playful
Are you a "ten-year" teacher that has taught one year ten times or a teacher with ten years of exploration under your belt? Playfulness involves letting go of worry and pressure and welcoming curiosity, spontaneity, and a sense of adventure. Many teachers need to play more, be more flexible, and say good-bye to their rigidity.

Start by looking for the humor in your inconveniences. Laughing at life's absurdities will reduce your stress, help you control your emotions, and lead to more joy. Humor can help you forget your problems and put a smile on your face. When dealing with a tough situation or problem, try to pause, detach yourself momentarily from the situation, and find the humor. Ask yourself, "Why am I taking life so seriously?" Life isn't permanent – no one gets out alive. In a hundred years, what difference will it make anyway? So lighten up! If a tornado blows off your roof, be like the guy who put up a sign saying, "Open House Today." You get to *choose* how to respond to every situation.

You serve as an important role model for your students as they develop their playfulness and individual senses of humor. Here are some ways you can have more fun in the classroom:

- Start class with a funny story or joke to illustrate a point or introduce a lesson.
- Begin a file of cartoons that relates to your lesson plans.
- Skim *Readers Digest* for applicable stories and examples.
- Use props or magic tricks to enhance learning.
- Involve your students in learning through fun role-plays and simulations.
- Present information in a game show format. If you're having fun, so will your students.
- Keep a list of funny things as they happen in your classroom and share them at appropriate times.
- Start a humor diary. Write down anything that strikes you as funny.
- Keep your eyes open for opportunities to place a joke or an anecdote in your lesson plan to reinforce a lecture.

Keep these things in mind:
- Be brief. Jokes have the greatest impact when you deliver them with brevity.
- Use variety. The unexpected creates anticipation.
- Be assertive. When you tell a joke, you should project confidence. Tell the joke from start to finish without pausing to see if you are amusing your students.
- Personalize jokes with your experiences. Or rewrite a joke with yourself, your family, class members, or school officials in place of other characters.

4. Practice Rehearsed Spontaneity.

If you've watched stand-up comedians at live performances, you were probably amazed you how quickly they can come up with responses to audience comments. For example, the comedian asks, "What do you do for a living?" An audience member replies, "Nothing," and the comedian responds without missing a beat, "Really? So how do you know when you're done?" (Bah-da-bump.) Most likely, the comedian has been in that exact situation before. He or she discovered a reply that worked, rehearsed the response, and made it appear spontaneous the next time someone made the comment. This is often called *rehearsed spontaneity*.

As teachers and parents, you run into the same situations from year to year. If you say something particularly funny, write it down and practice it! For example, if a student asks, "Are we going to do something important today?"

reply, "You're here, so I guess it's going to be an important day." This response is witty and builds the student's self-esteem at the same time. If a student asks, "Are you in a bad mood?" respond, "Now that you're here, I'm not," or "No, I'm sorry. I've made other plans." If your response strikes you as funny, use it again!

When you purposely look for, read, and collect this kind of humor, you will find that humorous thoughts and spontaneous, witty statements pop into your mind when you need them. Write down questions frequently asked by kids and run your answers by your friends and family. Try to listen differently to what your students tell you and look at life through their eyes. Respond with a new attitude that demonstrates curiosity. What's new? What's different?

5. Encourage students to tell funny stories that happen at home.

By sharing customs, rituals, and family stories from the home, students become more aware of the differences and similarities between cultures. They learn to accept one another and appreciate each person's uniqueness. You can ask your students:

- How do you celebrate birthdays and special events?
- What are some of your family traditions?
- What is the most important thing you have learned from your grandparents?
- Who are your heroes?
- What is the neatest gift you've ever received and why?

Sharing stories and revealing personal information validates the students and what they believe. It helps build a positive identity and a more favorable self-image. This is also a wonderful exercise to teach integrity, values, and cultural diversity.

Humor To Avoid

Knowing when to use humor is a skill that combines experience and intuition with a thorough knowledge of your students. Never use humor to:

- Tell racial jokes. The school is never a proper forum for sexist or racist humor or humor that fosters prejudice against females, ethnic minorities, religious groups, the elderly, or politics.
- Make fun of, ridicule, or embarrass students. Avoid sarcastic, flippant, or condescending remarks as an attempt at humor. Build your students up intellectually rather than tearing them down emotionally.
- Take up time. Humor should serve a specific purpose. Sometimes educators focus on the humor and not the educational value and learning. Use humor as a vehicle for learning rather than trying to be a stand-up comic.

A Final Word

It's so easy to go into "scold mode" and treat your students like children. "Don't do this...don't do that...act your age, will you?" These messages create tension and stifle communication. Students prefer a smiling and friendly teacher who has a sense of humor, because it demonstrates that the teacher is human and can share with the group. Humor creates rapport between you and your students, which is essential if you want your students to listen when you speak.

In ancient Jewish tradition, teachers would place dabs of honey on the pages of their students' books to make learning sweet. In time, this positive ritual would yield to the students' natural (and reinforced) love of learning. Positive humor will have the same effect. By creating an environment that fosters open, supportive communication, you will have receptive minds and greater learning. When used effectively in a classroom, humor can influence students to be more at ease with themselves and those around them. They are more willing to participate when they don't feel intimidated or embarrassed.

Anyone willing to take risks, engage the students, and apply the guidelines presented here can learn to use humor. Once you have formed a bond with your students, the learning begins and productivity is the end result. Remember, average teachers instruct, good teachers explain, great teachers illustrate, and the best teachers inspire through humor. After all, those who laugh, learn. If your students enjoy learning, they will want to "be there."

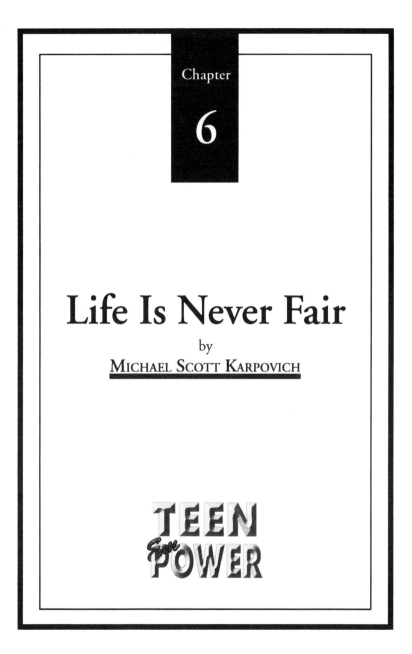

Life Is Never Fair

by
MICHAEL SCOTT KARPOVICH

TEEN
POWER

Life Is Never Fair

by
Michael Scott Karpovich

They say that "life isn't always fair"... don't believe them! Life is *never* fair!

I know what you're thinking... "What place does this chapter have in a book about empowering teens?" Well, if the truth be known, too often we set kids up for failure by suggesting that life is always good or that everything eventually works out – many times it simply doesn't.

Now don't get me wrong. I am not saying this *journey of life* isn't great – life *is* great, it is just hard. Personally, I am quite the optimist; indeed, my family calls me a *"Pollyanna."* But you must agree that irrational, unfounded optimism is different than practical, intelligent optimism.

If you say that "Life isn't always fair" what are you saying simultaneously? You're saying that "life is *sometimes* fair!" Now imagine the poor, desperate soul who doesn't fit in, who has a painful home environment, an alcoholic mother, a violent father, who is flunking classes, doesn't feel loved by anyone, and whose dog was just killed on the road... how does that person interpret that off-the-cuff remark?

If reality conflicts with what we are telling our kids, eventually kids come to the conclusion that either you and I are liars or that they, individually, are the one exception to the rule. I imagine this poor soul walking around wishing upon a star, waiting for life to "become fair"... and when they finally realize that life *isn't* fair, they conclude that they, unlike anyone else, never *deserved* anything good in their life.

The Else Factor

We have all heard people use the "*else factor*" – "Everybody else is happy!" "Everyone else has a good job." "Everyone else is popular." "Everybody else has more clothes." "Everybody else has someone that loves them!" "Everyone else has a happy family." You have heard teenagers say it again and again, and you know there have been times when we have said it ourselves. It is not simple jealousy or a feeling that the grass is always greener... actually, it is an unrealistic perception of "everybody else's" reality!

Reality is that everyone experiences adversity and pain; it is just that many hide it. Some hide their struggles because they don't want to bother anyone with their problems. However, most people hide their pain because they are ashamed! That shame comes from the perception that everyone else has it so much better than they do.

Once, during a keynote at a FHA/HERO conference, I listed different adversities we all face. I mentioned sexual abuse and told the young men and women that many of them had been abused, and they should "stop feeling so alone." I reassured them that I could not tell which of them had survived sexual abuse but (statistically) I knew that *many* of them had. After my talk, nearly a dozen students came to me and asked, "How did you know?" I explained to each of them individually that, statistically, the odds were against them. One boy said, "Yea sure, girls... but guys?" I responded, "More than you can imagine!" Anyone could see by his facial expression that he was saying with relief, "I am not alone!" No matter what our pain, we always feel that we are the only ones that have ever faced our particular issues. It is always a relief to realize that others are walking the same road (even if you never see them journeying next to you).

Jo Is Always Happy

Jo was one of those kids you long to have in your class. She was well behaved, cooperative and always smiled. I met her when I spoke at a teen leadership camp. She came to me and said she was going to kill herself. I was surprised and asked her "Why?!" She said, "Because no one understands, no one cares." I was shocked because Jo was obviously very popular. She had lots of friends, good grades and was successful in sports and, as far as I could see, she always *looked* happy. It was difficult to see her as suicidal! At home, it turned out that her father had abused her physically and emotionally. She hated him yet *couldn't* hate him because he was dying. I suspected that Jo was very upset that her friends couldn't see through her facade. It was the conflict of extremes of emotion that caused her to feel so desperate; her extreme positive feelings at school were cancelled out by her extreme negative feelings at home.

No one knew that Jo was sad because she didn't *look* sad. Her advisor told me, "Jo's always happy!" She was so good at hiding her shame and her pain that her teachers and friends had no idea that she was struggling. After we spoke, I did what every adult must do in this type of circumstance... I referred her to a school counselor who helped her get treatment. Jo was angry that I betrayed her feelings but a letter sent the next week told me she was relieved that "someone finally knew." Nevertheless, three years later (after graduating from high school as a straight "A" student), Jo took her own life. Everyone at her school was surprised.

We should never be ashamed of struggles – even the football star, beauty queen and valedictorian have their own issues to struggle through. It is just rarely obvious. When we realize that everyone goes through hard times – and many of us go through *very hard* times – we can begin to accept that although life is good, it is also hard, and certainly not fair!

We All Have a Mountain To Climb

Some will use the "else factor" and say that "Everyone else has less problems than I" or "Nobody else has to deal with problems like mine." In some cases, this makes a person feel special or even superior, but more often than not, it makes the person feel very alone.

Everyone has their mountain to climb. It is not for you or I to say that one person's mountain is steeper than another's – to each individual, theirs is just as steep as another's. Certainly, you can't compare a bad grade to child abuse, and who would ever suggest that a death in the family is the same as the loss of a pet; nevertheless, loss is loss, trauma is trauma and pain is pain.

Each person sees his own mountain as the highest to climb. What is needed is **perspective** – seeing our adversities as strengths rather than insurmountable mountains. Perspective involves a lot of time, work and patience. Rarely do we just come by it.

The Invisible Boy

When I speak at schools, I try to offer that elusive *perspective*. Often, my message to students is how to develop resiliency skills. I tell them how as a student I was the "nerd" that got beaten up and how that made me stronger in the end. "After all," I say, "nerds rule!" I share with them how adversity makes you stronger, or as I put it is... "Yuk Makes You Stronger!"

When I can, I like to sit with students before I speak. At a program in Boston, I sat near the back of the auditorium with the tenth graders. Most of the students didn't even notice me and those who did had no idea who I was or what I was doing there. This anonymity allowed me to feel the pulse of the school and the students. I listened to them talk and noticed how they interacted. I observed some who demanded attention and I saw some who did their best to be invisible.

One such "invisible boy" sat in front of me reading a textbook. Most kids ignored him but some started to tease him unmercifully. They called him a "dork" and a "nerd" and taunted him because he was wearing a crooked tie and slacks instead of jeans. One bully actually shoved him but it didn't seem to affect him. I turned to him and asked him how he could stand the way they were treating him. He looked at me with brown eyes that betrayed no emotion and said, "It's OK." "OK?" I yelled, "they were horrible. They teased you, they called you a nerd!" His facial expression did not change but those brown eyes took on a far off look and he said, "Today they call me 'nerd'... tomorrow they will call me 'boss.'" I patted him on the shoulder and laughed out loud at the brilliance of this tenth grade boy. His face remained expressionless but his very expressive eyes suggested that he was pleased with himself. I knew that even before I got up to speak that this "invisible boy" already had perspective. He already knew that in the end...NERDS RULE!

The Lambda Deltas

This "nerd" effectively demonstrated that sometimes the greatest adversities can be given new meaning. We have heard the child from a broken home who says, "Yeah... now I have two homes and four parents!" We smile sadly at their courage and marvel at their resilient perspective. They have reinterpreted the meaning of their struggle.

One day after an assembly at Meridian Middle School, I was asked to visit individual classrooms. One class was specifically designated for "learning disabled" children. I had spoken to a lot of special classrooms before but this one was different. There was a prevailing attitude of pride. Many of the students were wearing a cap or shirt with the Greek letters Lambda Delta printed on them. It was explained that this class was the "Lambda Deltas" because they were proudly *Learning Disabled!* They showed me photos of Tom Cruise and Whoopie Goldberg who were also proud "Lambda Deltas!" As I too was learning disabled, they presented me with a Lambda Delta shirt and inducted me into this proud fraternity. One of the kids from another class saw my new shirt and said, "I want to be a Lambda Delta, too!" One of the "Deltas" put his hand on the boy's shoulder and said, "I'm sorry – you can't be a Lambda Delta 'cuz you aren't learning disabled." I smiled. The teacher of this classroom had effectively turned a basically negative label into something to be proud of. This is how we all should treat our most painful situations – reinterpret the standard definition and give it an empowering meaning.

My Story

I mentioned that I was "learning disabled." In some ways, that is why I am a speaker for schools. Let me elaborate. Before I started kindergarten, doctors told my parents that I was brain damaged and recommended institutionalizing me. They said that I would never function normally in society. Lucky for me, my parents refused to accept this conclusion and took me to many doctors before one finally determined that I was either retarded or a genius. My parents decided to stop while they were ahead. Eventually, it was discovered that I had no depth perception, I was severely dyslexic, and I would regularly suffer from severe headaches. If I were in school today, they would have diagnosed me with attention deficit disorder and as learning disabled but in the early sixties, they didn't even have a handle on *dyslexia*!

My parents believed in me and pushed me to succeed but school was difficult scholastically and socially. From early on, I was the shy kid who was picked last for the team. Stunted growth combined with awkward social skills left me on the outside looking in.

Bullies were the only ones who picked me and they picked me as a favorite target. I was the class nerd and the kid they called "*stupid-dumb-retard.*" They didn't just beat me up – they found creative ways of doing it so I would be hurt physically and embarrassed emotionally. One time after Charlie and Rodney had finished shoving my head into a toilet (the kids call it a "swirley"), I cried, "Why do people have to be so mean?"

Eventually, I came to a crossroads. I had to either give up or develop a new strategy. I decided that I would no longer be a victim! Now for many people that means "fight back." I was never into violence and when you are shorter than all the other kids, it isn't too practical. I asked God for strength. I prayed a lot. I started to find things about myself that I genuinely liked. I decided to speak up, to laugh, to look at the "swirley" as a strength builder rather than a destroyer!

Finally, I figured out why people have to be so mean.... People are not mean because they are better than you; they are mean because they think you are better than they are. I was very short but to the bullies in school, I was bigger than they were. I was not popular but to them, I was more popular. I was brain damaged and I had to work very hard to do well in school but to them, I was smarter. Maybe, in my soul, I was always bigger, more popular and smarter than they were.

Now I speak to thousands because bullies stuck my head in toilets! One man called me up and asked, "Aren't you that guy that got flushed down toilets?" I asked him why he wanted to know and he told me he wanted me to come to his school and tell the kids how "yuk makes you stronger!" His school was on the island of Kauai! (The bullies thought they were sending me to the bottom of a toilet bowl – they were really sending me to Hawaii!) Perspective!

Almost every bully that beat me up ended up meeting an untimely end. I am sad because I wanted to thank them. A lot of what I have become as a person can be attributed to the strength and perspective they gave me. Then again, I really don't think I could have survived those painful years if it wasn't for my faith in God. To cope, I needed an eternal perspective. Unconditionally, every problem we face fades in that understanding. Unfortunately, I can rarely share this ultimate truth when I speak in public schools.

I started out this chapter telling you that life isn't fair...perhaps I was wrong. Perhaps the horrible events that we have *all* survived are our greatest advantages and therefore, in retrospect, are very fair. Perhaps we have mistakenly defined *"fairness"* as only happy, positive experiences, when in reality, fairness sometimes means we must go through painful character building experiences. Everyone struggles in life – some do it early, some do it later; the difference is if you struggle to fit in early in life, you never lose your drive. Unfortunately, if you struggle to fit in later in life, you may never find your drive. Whether it is fair or not, life isn't easy. Life is hard for every single person that breathes, but it is that difficulty that makes us strong.

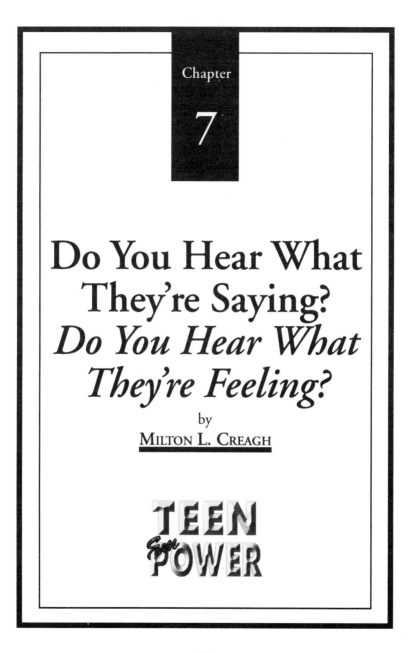

Chapter

7

Do You Hear What They're Saying?
Do You Hear What They're Feeling?

by
MILTON L. CREAGH

TEEN POWER

89

Do You Hear What They're Saying?
Do You Hear What They're Feeling?

by

Milton L. Creagh

Recently, I had one of those unfortunate, yet memorable experiences at the airport. For reasons beyond my control, I was running late for a flight to Orlando, Florida. My wife Henrietta dropped me off, and I ran as fast as possible (for someone forty with bad knees and 300 pounds to carry). I knew that everything would have to go just right for me to make it. (No, I did not show up one hour in advance as the airline recommended.) As I stood in the First Class line, things looked fairly promising. There were only two people in line in front of me. Twenty minutes later, I realized just how much of a delay two people can cause. To make a long story short, things did not go "just right."

When I finally got to the ticket counter, it was pretty obvious that I was going to miss my flight. Not only was I late and in a slow line, but the flight was leaving out of gate B-1, which in the Atlanta Airport is just about the furthest point from the ticket counter. Missing my flight created a major problem for me, because if I waited for the next flight, there was no way I could make it to Orlando in time for my speaking engagement. If this wasn't bad enough, the young lady at the ticket counter started making jokes about people missing flights. I didn't see the humor in her remarks. I knew it wasn't her fault but was offended by her sense of timing. I felt as though she didn't *hear* my feelings. It made me wonder what I had done to her. Couldn't she hear it in my voice? Or read the expression on my face that clearly said this was not a matter to be taken lightly? I didn't want her sympathy, but I did want a little respect for my feelings.

On the way home, my thoughts shifted from the ticket agent and settled on our children. In the middle of my drive home, it dawned on me that all too often, good, loving, committed parents and teachers do the same thing to their kids. By our action or inaction, we often take away their right to FEEL.

I annually speak to over half a million kids around the world. Normally, after I finish a session, a number of kids come up to talk one-to-one. It is truly amazing how often they mention that *no one listens to them*. My experience at the ticket counter helped me really understand how bad this feels. You see, I learned that when people don't *feel* heard, it doesn't matter if their words were *physically* heard or not.

I often ask kids, "*Have you ever been down in the dumps, either because you lost a girlfriend or boyfriend, or because somebody laughed at how you play basketball, or because you dress differently?*" The kids always loudly respond "YES!" Then comes my follow-up question, "*Have you ever tried to talk to your parents about what was bothering you and then got the $50 speech on how you 'Don't have any real problems because you're too young,' or 'Just wait until you're grown and paying bills?'*" The kids give a much louder response, "**YESSSSSSS!!!**" Then I ask my final question on the matter, "*So, do your parents answers make your problem go away? Of course not!*"

Mom, dad, why do we communicate with our kids like this? One of the best things that can happen to us as parents is to have the kind of relationship with our kids where they will freely talk to us. However, we often sabotage a part of our cherished relationship with our children very early in the game.

It almost seems as though we're playing *one-upsmanship* with our kids. Our grown-up problems are bigger, badder, and certainly more important than all their "kid stuff." Maybe, in the grand scheme of things, this is true. But our kids don't live in "the grand scheme of things." They live in <u>their</u> world, and <u>their</u> problems are real, big, bad, and very important. It would be bad enough if we simply compared their "kid-problems" to our "grown-up" problems, but sometimes we take it even further. We compare their problems to *our* <u>old</u> kid problems. And our current memory-based versions of our problems make us believe that ours were always bigger, badder, and tougher, and we always handled them better.

As a teen growing up on the southside of Chicago, I remember complaining about having to ride the subway for an hour and fifteen minutes just to get to school everyday. My father (not meaning any harm) promptly went into a lengthy commentary on how that was nothing, because back when he was a boy, he had to walk five or six miles to school everyday!

Now don't get me wrong. I love my dad and liked hearing some of his stories about the old days, but I needed him to help me deal with my situation. Maybe dad didn't see my problem as being as big as his because he was biased. He must have felt as though he already dealt with the "stuff" in his world. In his world, where he lived, his problems were the only ones that were real, big, bad, and important.

I wonder why we so often miss the golden opportunity to bond with our children as they are experiencing pain, heartbreak, and loneliness. These are wonderful teachable moments. Yes, you're correct when you tell them in the middle of their broken-heart trauma that they'll be crazy about someone else in the next 30 or 45 days, but that does not take away their current pain, hurt, or embarrassment. When humans experience pain, we try to find ways to relieve it. All too often our children opt to relieve their insecurities and fears with drugs and alcohol. *Wouldn't it be better if we took the time to teach our children how to deal with problems and not run from them?*

I was visiting with a group of kids in Florida a few years ago. We started talking about peer pressure and low self-esteem because they are the primary reasons kids put themselves in high-risk situations. One young man, John, told me that he thought the explanation was a lot more involved. He felt that adults often *over-simplified* the issue. When I asked him to explain, he shared with me a story. Apparently, John and a couple of his friends had been invited to a party, one of the first *real* teen parties he'd been invited to. He was excited and wanted to be there. He wanted to have fun, but most of all, he wanted to see Meg, a young lady he had a huge crush on.

When John and his buds rolled into the party, everything seemed to be swinging. There was alcohol and pot at the party, but John wasn't into drugs and had no intention of picking up the habit. He said he didn't feel any real pressure to use them. After he and his friends had drifted around trying to figure out what to do, he saw Meg. She was standing with a group of other people and swaying to the music that John had barely noticed. All of a sudden an idea raced through John's mind. Why not ask her to dance? Other people were dancing, and she looked like she was practically dancing by herself anyway. There was only one problem: John was not a dancer. He was convinced that if he tried to dance, everyone in the room would stop whatever they were doing to watch him make a fool of himself. While he was still trying to figure out what to do, one of his buds noticed him noticing Meg. His friends then started egging him on. They told him to go talk to her and dance with her. John knew they were his friends, but he also knew that if he went over to Meg now, they would watch the whole thing. If she didn't want to dance or talk to him, his friends would all die laughing! Eventually, John did approach Meg, but he stopped in the kitchen and visited the beer cooler first. He thought that if she refused to dance with him, he'd later tell his friends that he really didn't want to dance with her anyway – the beer had made him go over. He further thought that if he did dance and people laughed, he could also blame that on the brew. Besides, he'd also heard people call alcohol "liquid courage" and felt he needed some courage to make his move.

Amazing. John's situation, which started off rather innocently, led to what could have been a very dangerous ending. Ever since John relayed his story to me, I have shared it with kids all over America. Afterwards, I ask if they know anyone like John. Typically, 50-60% of the kids raise their hands. As a father of four, I often ask myself how

John would have responded in this situation if someone (preferably his parents) had taken the time to teach John how to deal with stressful situations.

Unfortunately, adults often teach kids to react in the way that John did. In effect, they model bad coping mechanisms to their children. For example, let's say someone comes home from a really lousy day at work. For that person, it's been the kind of day we've all had where you wish you'd win the lottery so you'd never have to face that job or those people again. As soon as that adult arrives home, he or she starts griping about *how bad their day was* and *how bad the traffic was* and *how the boss doesn't know their head from a hole in the ground!* Then, in the middle of the griping and moaning, that person asks their spouse, *"Baby, we got anything to drink in there? I need one bad."* If children observe this, what have they just learned from this lesson in problem solving? After all, kids have lousy days, too.

Whenever our children encounter a crisis, no matter what we think of the severity or lack thereof, we have an incredible opportunity to prepare them for life's trials and tribulations. Thank God that most of our children's traumas are not huge. They're not supposed to be. Their problems are supposed to be "kid problems," but those problems are the training ground for the bigger problems they will face as adults. If we don't help them learn to cope with the little struggles, how will they ever learn to deal with the big ones?

Parents, don't fool yourselves. Today's teens are carrying around some heavy baggage. Some are dealing with issues and stressors that you never had to think about at their age; and they shouldn't have to think about at their age. But the world has changed.

When we were kids, we didn't even know what AIDS was. Personally, I had never heard of bulimia or anorexia. Just a decade or two ago, only the major cities in America had street gangs, and those that did had little experience with the phenomena known as a "drive-by." Most of us spent considerable time with our extended families, and we lived in communities where everybody knew everybody. Today, many of us can't even name more than three of our own neighbors. When you and I were growing up, there wasn't any cable TV or video games, so we went outside to play when we got home from school. Today, kids spend their afternoons indoors, interacting primarily with a television, boom box, or computer.

I guess it all boils down to one concept: respect. I have to love my children enough to respect their issues. Although their issues may not be real, big, bad, important issues for me, they are very real, big, bad, important issues to them. I need to listen and hear what they are saying and what they are feeling. Only then can I be effective as a parent. Ironically...if the ticket agent at the airport had respected me enough to hear what I was feeling, this might never have occurred to me.

FAITH is Not a Four Letter Word

by
BILL CORDES

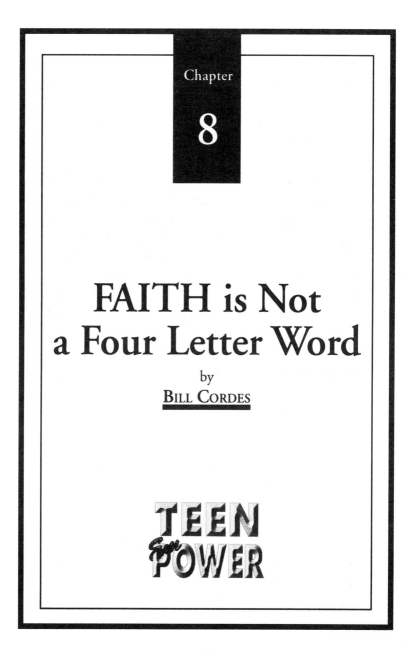

FAITH is Not
a Four Letter Word

by
BILL CORDES

The transitional phase between youth and adulthood called the teen years can be an exhilarating or exhausting experience and the difference that makes the difference for the teens in your life is YOU! I know it sounds like a lot of responsibility and I am not going to fluff you up by telling you that it is easy. Chances are you already know that being a role model for teens is the "toughest job you will ever love." However, I hope to give you some insights and reinforce a simple principle that you already know about called FAITH.

Before I do, I want you to remember the first time you decided that you were going to be a teen advisor, counselor, teacher, coach, social worker or parent. I want you to remember your optimism, how you were going to change the world or the first time you held that small baby in your arms and all the possibilities you experienced as you looked into his or her eyes. I want you to think about your hopes, dreams and that fresh exciting feeling of optimism you had when your vision was young.

I can remember what it was like for me when I first dreamed of being a high school teacher. I can remember how I yearned to have my own classroom. I can remember the energy, optimism and hope I had when I first walked into the teachers lounge on the first day of my teaching career. I can also remember how crushed I felt the first time a fellow teacher came up to me and said, "I use to be just like you, all full of energy, faith and hope ... wait a couple of years, you will change."

We have all been exposed to the loud speaking, negative preaching minority in the world that view "faith in teens" as a "dirty" phrase. Chances are if you are reading this you're like me, you did change. Your hope got stronger, your efforts became more efficient, success gave you more optimism and you still have within you the unshakable belief called faith. I know that you are proud of your faith in teens, and I want to support you in making some more distinctions about the *five letter word* we call faith.

My mother had faith in me, and it was a very quiet, unshakable faith that has forever molded my being. My mom is one of those people who still to this day is always upbeat and positive, and to be honest as a teen her positive attitude would get on my nerves. As an adult, I have grown to appreciate her and love her even more, but while growing up I would sometimes grow weary of her optimism. My mom would wake me up in the morning with annoying singing that would scare away animals and frighten small children. "Rise and shine sleepy head get out of bed another day ahead." My response was. "Mom...LEAVE ME ALONE." Still my mom continued to push, annoy, and stay positive about what was possible for me in my life.

My mother believed in me, and now I believe in myself. I never truly realized the impact of her subtle faith in me until I started having success, and now I see it as the true reason why I do what I do today.

When I was growing up, it seemed that nothing ever came easy for me. I struggled in school, struggled with friends, struggled with sports and always got into fights. My challenges came from being slow to gain confidence and from being around older siblings who seemed more talented than me.

My older brother, Tanis, was talented in everything. School came easier for him, he was faster, sharper, more quick-witted, and always seemed to be the center of attention. I always looked up to him, wanted to hang out with his friends and tried to do everything that he did. When I was 12, Tanis got a unicycle for his birthday. He took it out of the box, assembled it, and three days later he was riding it. He rode it to school and all over town. I thought that riding a unicycle looked pretty cool so I decided that I would like to learn. Some friends of ours had one hanging in their garage, so I bought it from them, and was hopeful and optimistic that three days later I would be riding the one wheeled monster.

Each day after school I would come home and try to ride it. It took me three days just to figure out how to even balance myself on it while holding on to my dad's truck. It was all I could do to let go of the truck for a split second without falling off. Three days turned into a week, and one week turned into two with no success.

One day after school I was out trying to ride and it seemed that I was getting worse not better. Some of the neighborhood kids had been by and razzed me a little about spending so much time trying to learn. They commented about how my brother had taken only three days to learn, and it seemed as it was taking me forever. I kept going with a little less confidence. I would start with the unicycle up next to the curb and about as far as I could get was 5 feet before I fell. After about an hour of this I threw the unicycle down, went into the house and was obviously upset. I had just about given up.

As I came into the house, throwing a little tantrum, my mom looked at me and said: "What's wrong?" I replied, "I can't ride that stupid thing." My mom said: "Well you will never learn sitting in here will you?" I said, "Mom, you don't understand, I can't get it. Other kids can do it because they are more coordinated than I am. Besides I don't even want to learn." She replied..." Well, lets do it again." I continued to be negative, probably trying to get attention. "Mom, I can't do it. I don't want to ride that stupid thing." My mom insisted, "Let's do it again!" We went out and she watched, and I was giving about half effort. Each time I attempted I would have some kind of excuse about why I was unable to do it. Still she persisted in her optimism, and was starting to wear on my nerves. "One more time, see how far you can go." In a pathetic victim, weak voice I replied, "OK I'll try."

All of the sudden my mom turned into Yoda from Star Wars: "Try, try... there is no try, only do or not do. Now, get up on it and see how far you can go!" I put in a half effort, fell off, looked and my mom and yelled, "SEE I CAN'T DO IT!" I then took my unicycle and threw it to the ground as hard as I could. As the seat of the unicycle hit the pavement it broke off.

We stood in silence, and my mom responded in optimism as I would expect. "I had no idea you were so strong." She turned, went back in the house and did not say another word. I almost felt a sigh of relief because the unicycle was broke and I was off the hook of learning to ride. Life was back to normal for me. My mom didn't say another word about riding the unicycle.

The next day, I was the first kid home from school, and was ready to come and relax while watching the Brady Bunch. As I walked through the front yard I glanced at my broken unicycle, and thought about how stupid I was to spend so much time trying to learn how to ride that dumb one wheeled contraption. I walked in the front door, past the kitchen table, and noticed a bag with my name on it. I looked inside the sack. It was a new unicycle seat.

I remember thinking, "Why did she do this to me?" I got a little upset at first, and then frustrated because it meant that my mom expected me to learn to ride the unicycle. I went to the door, looked out on the lawn at the broken unicycle. I looked back at the seat. Then I got angry and thought, "I know she expects me to do it, but I don't care because who needs to learn how to do that anyway...it's stupid" I turned on the TV, and tried to forget about it.

It seemed like the more I tried to ignore the seat the more I could hear my mom saying, "Let's see how far you can go." Finally, out of frustration I got a wrench and put the seat on the unicycle.

My attempts were different this time. I had more persistence because I knew that someone else had faith in me. I could feel the weight of my moms' expectations, but they seemed to empower me rather than discourage me. My mom came home, and saw me out in the street. I waved, she smiled, but neither of us uttered a word back to one another. My friends came by and said discouraging things, but this time what they said had no impact on me because I knew that I was doing this for me, and it did not matter how long it took.

A week later, after wearing holes in two pairs of jeans, and dealing with very sore thighs I was still going. I was seeing progress and knew that I would eventually get it.

Then it happened. I hopped on, took a deep breath and rode the unicycle all the way down the street, turned around a came back. When I finally fell I was so excited I wanted to yell. I looked around and realized that no one had seen my success. Just as I was about to get on the unicycle again my mom hollered from the porch, "Good job, I knew you could do it!" I smiled and waved.

Since I have become an adult my mom has confided in me about my learning to ride the unicycle. She said, "I was always a little concerned about you before you learned to ride the unicycle, after you learned to ride I knew that you were going to be OK."

She was right. She wanted for me what I want for my daughter, and what we want for the teens that we serve each day. We want them to be able to deal with adversity, and still have the courage to keep going. Because of my mom's faith in me I gained the confidence necessary to be persistent in my daily life. Her faith was subtle, unshakable and was expressed in her presence, actions and words.

I often hear people say, "these teens are different because they have no respect" or "I can't work with these teens because they have no morals or principles." I can't speak for their experience but I do know that teens today need what we needed when we were teens. They need love, encouragement, respect and they need to know that someone believes in them so they can believe in themselves.

The thousands of teens that I work with each year need to know what I expect of them and they need to know that I will not give up on them. Your teens need to know the same. If they believe that you will reach a point and give up, they will take you there just for the ride. If they believe that you are in it for the long haul then they know you have faith in them and that is an equation for a winning relationship.

F.A.I.T.H.

F = Forever Focused on a Vision.
As an educator it is important that we are forever focused on a vision. Let your teens know your dreams for them and for yourself. Allow teens to see you celebrating your success and failure so they will learn that it is not always easy. Teens today are bombarded with negativity from movies, media and peers. Sometimes negative influence can cause them to stray away from their goals. Your faith in them allows them to have faith in themselves. When we stand by them we support them in keeping their vision. We give them the courage to say, "Let's see how far I can go this time."

A = Always and in All Ways
Our motto as teen educators and role models should be, "We teach teens to look for the good always and in all ways." When bad things happen to good people we must be the role model for finding the greatness in those moments. However, don't expect teens to always react posi-

tively toward your optimism. Just as I acted as I didn't care about my moms support, your teens may act the same. It was just an act. Know that your faith and optimism is planting seeds for them to always look for the good when they fail. We have redefined mistakes in our family. We call them "great moments" because it gives us an opportunity to always find the good in all ways.

I = Integrity
Integrity is the quality or state of being of sound moral principle; uprightness, honesty and sincerity. It is also the state of being whole, complete or unbroken. As educators, we must set the standard of being whole and complete. While we still may be growing and learning it is important that we do so while we are living as our word and according to strong principles. We get into trouble when we ride the fence or become "wishy-washy." Let your teens know where they stand with you so they know what you expect.

T= Trust
Keep in mind that there is a difference between faith and trust. Faith is an unquestioning belief in your teen. Trust is an earned commodity and your teen must learn to trust you just as you must learn to trust your teen. You may not trust your teen but you can have faith in their ability to earn that trust. It is important for us as role models to sometimes back off and trust teens to learn to deal with adversity on their own. My mom gave me the space to

deal with adversities, but was there when she was needed. I am sure that she wanted to be right by my side every step of the way, but she knew that if I learned to deal with failure now it would save pain in later life.

H=Hope

Sometimes when we work with teens hope is all we have and many times it is all that is needed. Hope suggests an anticipation or expectation of what we want to happen. It was my mothers expectation or hope that I would ride the unicycle that motivated her to buy the unicycle seat. Her hope and expectation created desire in me to not let her down. Hope can go a long way, and it usually needs to be accompanied by words and actions to get the greatest results. Hope and expect that your teens will do the right thing and follow it up with words and actions.

Failure: Breakfast of Champions

by
CLARE LAMERES

Failure: Breakfast of Champions

by

CLARE LaMERES

Michael Jordon of the World Champion Chicago Bulls basketball team is seen striding through the back hallways of the stadium. His overcoat swings from side to side as he glides forward with the self-assured confidence of a winner. The voice-over we hear in this television advertisement is Michael's:

> *I've missed more than 9000 shots in my life.*
> *I've lost over 300 games.*
> *Thirty six times I've been trusted to take the game winning shot. . .and missed.*
> *I have failed over and over again in my life.*
> *And that is why. . .I SUCCEED!*

Wow! The message couldn't be any clearer! This fifteen second commercial succinctly illustrates valuable life attitudes that are held by successful people; important attitudes that I believe teachers and parents alike must teach to today's adolescents.

Failure has value!
Success comes from failure!
It is okay to fail: it is not okay to give up!

Imagine what our world would be missing if Thomas Edison had given up after his first unsuccessful experience with electricity; if the Wright Brothers had given up after their first failed attempt at flight; if Elizabeth Cady Stanton and Susan B. Anthony had given up after their many defeats in attempting to secure the right for women to vote; or if Martin Luther King had given up after he was told that his "Dream" was impossible? The fact is, every wonderful invention, every widely held positive belief turned into positive action is the direct result of someone who did not give up.

The business world frequently complains to educators, *"You send us brilliant 4.0's who are afraid to take risks."* Well of course they are afraid to take risks: they have been told to avoid failure at any cost! Ask any "at risk" student about the cost of failure. Failure is such a recurring part of "at risk" students' lives, they actually see themselves as "nothing but losers." Where and when do young people today learn that failure is a reality in life and that there are ways to benefit from it?

Adolescence is a time when life attitudes are being formed and re-formed daily. Young people are searching for who they are, and most importantly, they are searching for how to live. They use various "costumes" and hairstyles in attempts to "try out" different ways of "being." These are cosmetic and transitory statements about their attitudes of the moment. The important attitudes, however, the ones that will stay with them for the rest of their lives, the attitudes that will impact their contributions to the world, these are the attitudes that concerned educators and parents must help young people explore and develop.

One such important life attitude that we can teach is **how to deal effectively with failure.** Successful people understand the importance of looking for the valuable lessons in their experiences because they believe that these lessons will eventually lead to success. They do not hold on to failures; they hold on to lessons. They understand that the failure is the hard packaging around an event, a selection on life's menu. The lesson inside that failure, on the other hand, is a powerful source of nutrition supplying them with the energy they need to move toward success.

The lesson that follows is similar to many other such activities found in my book, The Winner's Circle: Yes, I can? Self-Esteem Lessons for the Secondary Classroom. It includes parts that are actually scripted for you. Obviously, you do not have to use this exact script. You may prefer to use it as a model as you tailor your remarks to your own situation and style. This lesson is designed to teach adolescents how to reframe failure and how to see the value in a negative situation. I believe this is a powerful ability that will serve them well for the rest of their lives as they go forth to make their indelible mark on this planet. I call this lesson:

THROW AWAY THAT FAILURE

TIME: The time needed for this activity is 10 to 15 minutes or more, depending upon how much discussion you wish to encourage. The activity is not a one-time experience. I suggest you use it frequently in your classroom or home, at least once a week!

Introducing the Lesson:

After putting students into pairs, tell them that you are going to pose a question which they will discuss with their partners for approximately 30 seconds. Before they begin, emphasize that there is no <u>one</u> "right" answer to the question, many possibilities will come to mind. Now, the question:

Why do some people fail to get what they want in life?

After 30 seconds ask for class "shares" and record them on the board. Acknowledge and discuss these responses, pointing out that everything recorded on the board is true (assuming it is). Next, while writing the following statement on the board, tell students that the <u>number one</u> reason people fail in life is **"fear of failure!"**

Next say:

How would you like to learn a technique that would guarantee you that fear of failure will not prevent you from getting what you want in life? Now, I need to warn you. Very few people know about this; in fact, only successful people know and use this secret.

Teaching the Concept:

Instruct students to take out a piece of notebook paper and tear it in half.

Ask students to think of a time in their lives when they failed – a time when things did not turn out the way they had hoped. The failure might be something they did not do but wish they had done. Clarify that it makes no difference what kind of failure they call to mind. Maybe they remember something that happened in the third grade, or perhaps the failure is recent. Did they forget to put the trash out yesterday, and now they are grounded? Did they fail to make the cut on the team? Did they tell a "half-truth" and make a bad situation worse? Did they wait too late to study for an exam?

Instruct students to take one of the half sheets of paper. Then in approximately 30 seconds, have them jot down a word or a short phrase that brings back the memory of the failure. There is no need to write out details of the incident. Stress that they will not be sharing this information with anyone else in the room.

Next, tell students to think about what they learned from this failure. Point out that we always learn something from our failures, even if it is, *"I'm never going to do that again!"* Maybe they learned to leave a note on the bedroom door as a reminder to put out the trash. Maybe they learned to set up a study schedule to follow as they prepare for the next exam.

Instruct students to use the other half of the paper to describe the lesson found in this failure. Suggest that they do this in just a few words or a short phrase, such as, "leave a note" or "study according to a schedule." Give the students 15-30 seconds to write this "lesson."

Explain to students that the value of any failure is the positive lesson it holds, the lesson that improves one's life. For example, if a student has written, "I'm a loser," as the lesson, he or she needs to keep thinking. That is not the lesson! The lesson may well be that the student <u>will lose</u> if he or she does the same thing again, which means that the real lesson is to "consider consequences before taking action." Ask the students to take an additional minute to consider what they have written as their "lesson" to see if they have truly found the message that will improve their lives.

Next instruct students to pick up the piece of paper on which they have written the failure. Model what you want the students to do by holding a half sheet of paper in front of you. Crumple it into a ball while saying:

> *Now, do this to your failure* (crumple, crumple). *Hold on to it because on the count of three, you are*

going to have a faaantasssy come true! You are going to get to throw something at the teacher! PULEEZ wait for my signal. (Cover your eyes to protect them.) *One, two, three, go!*

["Are you out of your ever-lovin' mind, Clare? I am not going to encourage students to throw something at me!" Alright, already! If you feel it is dangerous or downright disrespectful to let students throw the failure at you, then don't do it. Just put a waste basket in an accessible place and use <u>that</u> as the target. I've done the activity both ways. In real life most of the failures don't make it into the basket, nor do they hit me. Most of them miss, but not all, of course! An important component of this activity is the throwing motion. Students are embedding a physical memory here of literally throwing that failure away!]

Processing the Concept:

1. The next step is to ask students to process what they have just done. Say to them:

> *Consider the message in this activity. What do successful people do with their failures in life? They THROW THEM AWAY! What do they keep?* (Let the students respond with the answer...then you can repeat it.) *They keep THE LESSON!! Successful people clearly understand that the "lesson" in failure is actually a "gift." It is something they may not have learned had they not experienced that failure.*

Think about the message in this Mark Twain quote: "Once a cat sits on a hot stove lid, he will never sit on a hot stove lid again, and that is good. However, he will never sit on a cold one either." How are successful people unlike the cat in this quote? (Take some class "shares.") *Successful people do not quit just because they have a bad experience. Even when they fail the first time out, they are still not afraid to try something a second, third, or even a fourth time.*

Michael Jordan didn't give up playing basketball after he was cut from his high school basketball team. Walt Disney didn't give up "creating" after going bankrupt five times. Thomas Edison didn't give up trying to harness electricity after he failed to do so thousands of times. Babe Ruth didn't give up playing baseball even though he had more strike outs than any other player in baseball history. Elizabeth Cady Stanton, Susan B. Anthony, and thousands of other women did not give up fighting to win the right to vote even though they were challenged at every turn. Martin Luther King did not give up believing in his "Dream" of a nation where all men are treated equally even though his efforts were met with violent resistance. Why should you give up? Why not adopt the powerful life attitude held by every single successful person throughout the history of humankind:

"It is okay to fail; it is not okay to give up!"

2. Instruct students to turn to their partner and share an example of a valuable lesson learned from experiencing a failure. This example could come from their own life, the life of a friend, a family member, or even a famous or fictional character. Give students approximately one minute to do this, then ask for class "shares."

3. Suggest to students that they start seeing the lessons in their failures as "gifts of knowledge," knowledge that can help them become more successful human beings. Acknowledge that they may not be willing to accept the "lesson/gift" immediately. They may need time to process the hurt or the anger surrounding the failure before they are open to seeing its value. This waiting period is perfectly normal, perfectly "human." At the same time, encourage students to start consciously using the technique they have just learned. Say:

> *From this day forward, when you experience a failure, take the time to discover the "lesson." It will __always__ be there. You wouldn't want to overlook such a powerful gift!*

4. Special Note: It is important to emphasize to students that <u>changing directions does not necessarily mean one is giving up</u>. If the ship is actually going under water, one should jump! If the breakfast milk is sour, one should discard it! Explain that in many instances, it may be advisable to change directions and adjust one's course. While this might look like failure to others, only the student

knows for sure. Maybe he or she is just "backing up to get a running start!" As part of this lesson, or at a later date, you may want to have students partner up and discuss instances when they changed directions in order to ultimately experience success.

Keeping The Activity Alive:

Once a week, do this activity during the last five minutes of class. Repeating the process will give students numerous opportunities to discover even more powerful lessons they can use to move forward in life.

Reserve a space on your bulletin board and call it "BREAK-FAST OF CHAMPIONS." Encourage, or require, students to bring "successful failure" stories to class, stories that tell of success coming out of failure. Display these on the bulletin board all year and just keep adding to them. The stories, or portions of stories, can be xeroxed out of magazines or newspapers. If the story has been seen on television or heard on the radio, a written synopsis can be used.

This activity requires students to focus on people who do succeed. Surprisingly, these stories are everywhere! Although their positive subject matter is never the main course on the media's menu, you will be amazed how many of these stories your students will find. Participating in this assignment encourages students to be on the lookout for the positive side of living. It helps them to realize that,

"Yes, people do fail; this is a fact of life." The activity also helps them to see that successful people handle failure in a way that serves them. Most importantly, this activity inspires your students to model these "successful failures."

Student Reactions:

You will be gratified and inspired by students' reactions to this activity. Understandably, they are fascinated by the message. After all, many of them have spent the majority of their lives being told that failure brings shame; failure is unforgiving; failure is to be avoided. Now they are learning there is actually some value to failure. Their appetites for "positive risk-taking" will increase as the power of this message is translated into the reality of their own lives. As your students become more and more proficient at searching for those positive lessons, they will come to understand that failure truly is "The Breakfast of Champions!" Bon appétit!

Foundations
For Life

by
BOB LENZ

TEEN
POWER

Foundations For Life

by

BOB LENZ

As you begin to read this chapter, you may be wondering, Bob <u>Who</u>? I never heard of the guy!!! Actually, I used to think "who" was my last name. Before you skip to the next chapter, let me share with you why I was asked to write for <u>TEEN EmPOWER</u>. I am an expert at raising teenagers!

I bet you've already thought of a catch phrase for me: "Bob Lenz – Internationally Unknown **and** Arrogant." You may have even dismissed me with the conclusion that I probably don't even have teenagers. You are right! That's exactly my point. The only way to be an expert at raising teens is to not have any of your own. Once you have your own, everything you thought you knew goes out the window. Hang on, you are on the ride of "The Adolescent Roller Coaster." Our oldest daughter, Amber, turns 13 in September 1997. I have to write this chapter while I'm still an expert.

All joking aside, parenting and working with youth is tough. Don't get me wrong; it's one of the greatest joys in life. However, you will experience heartache and pain as they struggle through tough choices. Investing in youth takes thought, time, hard work, hugs, prayers, love, support and sacrifice.

Teen surveys still give MOM & DAD the top spot as to why kids stay drug-free. No one can take the place of parents! With that in mind, I humbly share a few observations to encourage you in your joyful struggle of parenthood. Through it all, remember that you are not alone! Parents, teachers, coaches, friends, neighbors, and clergy need to join together to build teens up so they can turn drugs down.

Foundations for Life

Because we want what is best for our teens, we try to build their lives or "houses" for them. We especially struggle over who is going to do the decorating. In the 90's, the battle ground has moved from the teen's closet to the teen's body. The battle lines are drawn on what they can pierce, if they can get a tattoo and what hair color they can have.

However, it's not the decorating I want to focus on today. I want you to examine the foundation. When their lives are built on a sound foundation, there will be security and safety in the midst of the storms of life. This solid base will also enable them to build their lives and destinies long after they have left our homes.

Foundation #1: Sense of Assurance

This first foundation is a sense of purpose that says, "I matter. My life counts. I have gifts and talents and was

CREATED for a reason." This self-confidence is important as the world rapidly changes around a teenager. Listen to your own heart, still longing for assurance in your job, marriage, friendships and finances.

A sense of assurance comes through <u>acceptance and unconditional love</u>.

I was struck by the importance of parental acceptance and love when hearing the story of a girl I met at a conference. She was a high achiever who was student council president and on her way to becoming valedictorian. She was involved in her school, church and community. She had chosen to be drug and alcohol free throughout her high school years. At some point in her senior year, the stress and pressure became too much for her. She made an unwise decision to drink. She came home at 1:00 a.m., feeling terrible and crying. She didn't want to wake her parents, so she sat out on the porch. Moments later, the door opened and there stood her dad. This may not seem unusual to you, but he was still in his underwear. (A father's underwear hangs down to his knees.) "What are you doing?" he asked. When he saw her crying, he sat down next to her. The dam holding back her tears broke. "Dad, I don't care. I just don't care if I'm valedictorian. I don't care if I get to the college you went to. I don't care if I get scholarships. I'm sick of the pressure!!"

She told me her dad put his face down in his hands and rubbed his head. For him, this was a gesture of disgust that was usually followed by punishment or lecture. He surprised her when he looked up with a tear in his eye and said, "I'm proud of your accomplishments and I want what's best for you. I hope you go to my alma mater and are the top of your class. But even if you don't, and even if you take a path I wouldn't choose for you, there's one thing you always need to remember: you'll always be my girl. I love you and I accept you."

"Really Dad? Really?" she asked. He nodded with a warm smile of approval. She left that encounter with her dad with an assurance that she was loved.

She quit school, moved out and went on welfare...to the contrary! She continued to excel. It doesn't always turn out this way, and there are no guarantees. Her father laid a sense of assurance as a foundation that she could build her life on.

There are two philosophies to choose from, "I do therefore I am" or "I am therefore I do." You can choose to live to try to find an identity or to live from a sense of identity. One produces human "doings" who base their identities on what they do. They build two-story lives with decorations galore. However, when hard times come, the foundation crashes. The other philosophy produces human "beings" who base their identities on the fact that they are a creation of God and are treated with love and acceptance. Foundation #1: Sense of Assurance, comes through acceptance and love.

Foundation #2: Sense of Belonging

Webster's Dictionary defines belonging as having a close, secure relationship. Teens tell us that the number one reason they join gangs is for a sense of belonging. They long to have other people take interest in them and feel concern for them. They are searching for a sense of connection, oneness and unity. I penned the following poem after listening to youth who were hurting:

MOM, ARE YOU HOME? DAD, ARE YOU HERE?

I really had something to share.
I just needed to know that you care.

The lights were on, but no one was home.
Nothing to do, I'll just hit the streets and roam.

New jeep and car, and of course the three-story house.
But what good is it when it's as quiet as a mouse.

People tell me I shouldn't complain, that I have it made.
I just wonder if that gang would accept me if I had a blade.

Well, it's somewhere to be, something to do.
Wow, know what, Mom and Dad? Now I hardly even think about you.

Sports!? Don't give me that! I'm not good enough. I got cut.
With these guys I'm in if all I do is sleep with a slut.

Dad, it's not that bad, she's a person too.
And who are you to talk? What if I told Mom what I knew?

Huh? You've worked hard to give me a good family?
What family? You don't even know me.

School called? Big deal; so I dropped out.
Kind of like you with the father/son outing in Boy Scouts.

I'm breaking Mom's heart? I don't care what she feels.
It's too late, I got the cards and now it's my deal.

Yeah, Dad, it's drugs. Want some?
I'm into sales. You'd be proud if you saw my income.

Who gives a rip what your friends think?
You're a puppet to people. It's sad and I think it stinks.

Don't tell me what to do.
I'm out of here! I don't need this house, your car,
your money. I don't need you!

Mom are you home? Dad are you here?
I really had something to share.
I just needed to know that you care.

This sense of belonging that teens are craving is best ac-
complished within the family. It also occurs in church,
youth group, friendships, communities, school, leagues,
team sports, clubs and classes.

A sense of belonging comes from <u>being involved</u>. There is
no substitute. You can't buy involvement, teach it or get it
from TV, computer, or even the Internet.

I had to come to grips with this when one of my daughters asked, "Daddy, why do you like speaking more than you like being with us?" What could I say? "Because the audience claps and sometimes I get standing ovations. If just once when I walk in that door, you and your mom would get off the couch, stand up and applaud, I would stick around more." No, I had to face the facts. I needed to love my daughter enough to lay the foundation of a sense of belonging. How? By being there. Love is still spelled T-I-M-E. The teachers, coaches, pastors, and parents who are making a difference are investing time. Foundation #2: Sense of Belonging, comes from being there.

Foundation #3: Sense of Confidence

It's easy for youth to be strong when they are in the majority. To be secure in their beliefs and morals when they're alone in a crowd is a different story.

On a Friday night, when even their close circle of friends make choices they don't believe in, do they have the confidence to stand up for what they believe and who they are? Do they make the right choice even when they know it will cost them popularity? Do they have convictions that remain when Mom, Dad or authorities are not present? If yes, that's a sense of confidence.

Confidence comes from criticizing adolescents' every move so they can improve. No, that's not it. I wish it was! My kids would have immovable confidence. Rather, confidence comes through <u>compliments</u>. Sometimes, adults need to look hard or dig deep to come up with a compliment. I challenge you to take some valuable time to write out all the characteristics you appreciate about your teen. Be specific and share warm memories you have with your son or daughter. Once, I was commenting to my dad about how bad I was in baseball, to which my dad responded, "Bob, you weren't that bad."

"Yes, I was Dad," I told him. "It's okay, I can handle it now."

"Bob, you weren't really that bad. One year, you were the last guy to get cut," he told me. We all laughed and agreed dad didn't need any help in compliments.

Youth need compliments from us or they will find it from their peers. If praise comes from their friends, their confidence will be connected to the approval of the group. If compliments come at home, they will have deep seeded confidence in themselves that they can build their decisions and life upon. Foundation #3: Sense of Confidence, comes from compliments.

Foundation #4: Sense of Dignity

It was the first day of the school year. I was waiting in the gymnasium as the 6th, 7th, and 8th graders herded in for the assembly program. A seventh-grade girl was dressed in black on this blistering hot August day. She had big bold letters on her shirt that read, "**DO ME.**" My heart cried as I imagined the pain, anger, fear or emptiness screaming out behind her facade. This young girl is a picture of the opposite of a sense of dignity. This is rampant in some pockets of our youth culture today. There is a lack of respect for self, property, parents, authority and life itself.

Dignity is a sense of worth and honor. This does not come from letting teens explore their individuality at any costs. Today, many people teach that there are no absolutes and no rights and wrongs. I believe that theory is absolutely wrong! People are fighting for personal rights instead of **what is right**. This is why I believe a sense of dignity comes through <u>discipline</u>.

Youth will not be responsible until they are held responsible. Some people may have a primitive view of discipline that equals punishment. That's not what I'm talking about. I'm talking about youth facing consequences for their choices to show them that their decisions count. As youth develop into adults, it is necessary to train them to make wise choices. If they feel they can get away with any kind of behavior, they, and society, are in for a rude awakening.

I met a principal who was at wits end about prevention. He adamantly said he couldn't do it alone. He went on to tell a story about ten guys who skipped out of school. After questioning them one at a time in his office, nine guys confessed they had been drinking at John's house. He brought in the last guy, John. He said he was home sick. The principal said, "John, we know. The other guys told all." John acted surprised, "I was home sick. If you don't believe me, call my mom." The principal called her. Guess what? She said John was home sick. She lied for him! She thought she was being a "cool" parent, when in fact she was stealing his sense of dignity. By not disciplining him for his actions, she lost a chance to teach him a valuable lesson under her loving guidance. John will never be what he was meant to be or deserves to be. When external discipline is absent while a child is growing up, internal discipline will never be developed. Without internal discipline, teens can not reach their destiny or fulfill their dreams. Instead they will live with regret and mediocrity.

This is an area with which I still struggle. Even as I finish this chapter, I look out the window and the sky calls my name and the nearby lake beckons me. I also hear another voice in my head, a football coach from seventh grade. At practice, I was jogging during sprints. Coach Romenesko yelled, "Lenz, pick it up." "It hurts," I whimpered. He barked back, "If it doesn't hurt, it doesn't help!" Cruel? No! Discipline! This built a solid foundation, because it came from a coach who was my caring, compassionate and disciplined teacher. He wanted the best for me.

As an adult, I continue to build a sense of dignity that comes through discipline. As I complete this writing project, I enjoy a feeling of accomplishment. After I put down my pen, I'll gather my children and say, "Kids, let's go fishing...but first we have to cut the lawn." To which they will respond, "Daaaaaaaaaaaaaaad. That's no fun!" Excuse me. I have to go lay a foundation.

Packing for Success
Preparing for the Future

by
JIMMY CABRERA

TEEN
POWER

Packing for Success
Preparing for the Future
by
JIMMY CABRERA

O ne morning, I was sitting at the kitchen table next to my daughter's backpack. As I sat there pondering and planning my activities for the day, I could not keep my eyes off the backpack. After a few moments, it came to me. I stood up and thought, "That's it! Our 'backpack' will determine our success."

I realized that morning that what we put in our "backpack of life" prepares us for our future and dictates our future success. As adults, we have been stuffing our backpacks with either negative or positive tools. In every situation of our lives, when we need a particular tool to move forward, we reach into our backpack and pull out a tool. Positive or negative, the outcome is a direct result of what we have previously put in there.

This backpack metaphor is relative to all youth. The backpack is something that is tangible for each young person to relate to and draw from. As a professional speaker, I have developed a presentation to encourage and help young people prepare for the future by giving them some tools (ideas) they can put into their backpacks. Taking the word, "BACKPACK," I will give you eight points you can teach and encourage young people to "put" in their backpacks.

B A C K P A C K

"B"ACKPACK: "_B_elieve in myself" is the first thing to place in one's backpack of life. It is the foundation of success. Teach every young person to pack a lot of belief in themselves. Self-esteem is critical to one's journey to success. We must incorporate positive "self talk" in our lives. As our youth go through life, they will find it necessary to pull belief in themselves from their backpack to survive and experience success in today's world.

One of the most frequent questions I am asked is, "What motivates a person?" My response is simple. The key to motivation is one word, "Believe." Believe comes from two English words, "by" and "live;" therefore, the key to motivation is to "live by something." If an individual is not motivated, that person is not living by anything. Teach each youth to choose something positive to live by – finishing school, making the honor roll, finishing college, being a good friend, etc. Living by this "something," one will do whatever it takes to achieve it.

As we continue to believe in ourselves, let us teach our youth to place 'pride' in their backpacks. I am not speaking of arrogance or some type of inflated ego. I am talking about teaching them to be "proud" of their heritage, to never be ashamed of who they are, where they live, or anything else that may keep them from moving forward.

I was reared in a small town in north Texas in the 60's; my family was labeled different. In fact, we were the first Latinos (Mexicans) allowed to attend the public schools. It was a time when the only people who promoted my well being and encouraged me to succeed were my parents. Yes, we did experience prejudice and rejection, but we survived and succeeded. My parents taught us to always be proud and walk with our head held high.

One day I was having some challenges with a few of my classmates. They put me down, picked on me, and called me names. My mom said, "Mi hijo (son), no one in this town or country is better than you." But, she did not stop there, she continued by adding, "…and you are no better than them, for we are all equal in God's eyes. Be proud of yourself and always walk with your head up." Since that day my backpack has been loaded with pride, respect, and the determination to always do my best in whatever task I am given.

Twenty-four years ago, I learned ten two-letter words, from a speaker named Cavett Roberts, that have made an impact in my life. Please etch them in your mind and heart: "If it is to be, it is up to me." Think of them with your fingers, one word for each finger. Every time you look at your hands, remember, "If it is to be, it is up to me." In

English, it is ten words, but in Spanish, only seven, "Si tiene que ser, depende de mi." The meaning is the same in all languages.

B"A"CKPACK: *A*ttitude is everything. In our backpacks, we need the right attitude to ensure success. We need to develop a positive attitude about school, teachers, peers, authority, character, integrity, nutrition, exercise, truth, commitment, believing in oneself, and much more. Take two sports teams that are basically equal in stats, records, size, etc. There can only be one first place winner in the end, so what separates these two teams? It comes down to the team that is "better" prepared mentally. The team with the right *attitude* wins. This scenario can be applied to our lives. The "team" with the best attitude, and which is most adequately prepared, will win.

I learned the following from a fellow speaker and friend. How many letters are there in the alphabet? Answer: 26. Each letter of the alphabet has a corresponding number. The "A" is the 1st letter and the "Z" is number 26. Now take the word "Attitude," and identify the corresponding numbers for each letter: A=1, T=20, T=20, I=9, T=20, U=21, D=4, E=5. Add these numbers together, and you will find they add up to 100. Always have your backpack ready with a 100% positive attitude, for attitude is everything.

BA"C"KPACK: *C*ourage. In our backpacks we need to carry unlimited amounts of courage. Why courage?

COURAGE to stand firm for one's values; say no to alcohol, tobacco, drugs; believe in oneself; maintain a positive attitude; stay in school; always do your best; respect authority; voice your opinion; and the list goes on. One must possess the courage to ask for *help*! You haven't experienced success until you feel free to ask for help.

BAC"K"PACK: *K*nowledge. You may be familiar with the phrase, "Knowledge is power." Let me add one word to the phrase, "*Applied* knowledge is power." We may acquire all the know-how and savvy, but it will not do us any good until we apply what we know. We must teach our youth that one obtains knowledge through continuous education.

When it comes to knowledge, enlighten every young person that individuals get paid for what they know. In some of the assemblies where I present to youth, I teach them this lesson. Midway through the presentation, I ask, "Can one student here today name the last five presidents of the United States?" I reward the first student to come up with the right answer with a twenty dollar bill. Then, all of the sudden, all the students want to answer my questions! I assure you, the students will not soon forget that people pay you for what you know.

Some of the best advice I ever received was from Walt. At the time, Walt was 94 years of age, I asked him to what he would contribute his success. Walt, in his straight forwardness, looked up at me and said two words, "Remain Teachable." Then he got up, and walked away. Thank you, Walt, for giving such great wisdom for my success.

I encourage all students to always try, and in trying, do their best. When it comes to trying, many are afraid of failure. Adults, too, experience this fear. Therefore, we must teach all individuals that failure is okay. Mom, dad, or teacher, if I were to go up to your child or student and ask them if failure was okay, how would they answer? In an assembly format, with anywhere from 40 to 4,000 students, I ask them this question. Less than 10% of the group will agree that failure is okay. Never allow a child to grow up without acknowledging the fact that without some failures in life, there are no successes. Master the phrase, "I never see failure as failure, but only as learning experience." Every experience provides us a lesson to learn from and should encourage us to continue trying.

When my son, Marcus, was nine years old, I heard some commotion, and followed the noise. I walked into the garage, and I could tell Marcus was considerably upset. He was throwing all his tools against the wall of the garage. I tried to get his attention, "Marcus, what's going on, dude?"

He responded, "Look, Dad, I tore apart my bicycle, and then I put it back together, and *look*, I have extra parts!"

"Okay, Marcus, say it."

"I don't want to, Dad."

"Say it, Marcus."

"Okay, Dad...'I never see failure as failure, but only as a learning experience.'"

"Good, Marcus. Now, what did you learn?"

Crying and frustrated Marcus said, "I learned how not to do it."

I handed him the manual, and walked away. Why? Well, I certainly had no clue how to fix it.

Two hours later I looked out the window and saw Marcus riding up and down the street on his bike. Did Marcus learn a lesson? Yes, he did, and if that is the only lesson he has learned from me, praise God, for Marcus will be very successful.

BACK"P"ACK: *P*eople Skills. People skills can be developed and ready to be pulled out of one's backpack. Our youth needs to be taught to get along, and how to work together in harmony. There is one characteristic I would like every individual to secure in their backpack: "Respect." Let us recall the old adage, "People don't care how much you know until they know how much you care." From my experiences in working with people, I have found that "respect" ensures successful relationships.

BACKP"A"CK: _A_lways set goals in your life and career. It is never too early or too late in life to set positive goals. It is a process, and every individual can learn steps of setting goals.

The following survey caught my attention. There were 10,000 individuals interviewed in reference to setting goals. The results came back as follows: 3% responded by saying that they "write" their goals down; 17% responded with, "We 'think' about our goals;" 60% said, "All we care about is living 'week to week'" (Isn't this sad?...Do you know what happens when you just live "week to week"? You become "we_a_k."); 20% responded with, "All we care about is 5 p.m. when we get off work." The survey concluded by saying that the 3% that wrote their goals down became 50% to 70% more successful. I encourage you to set goals and have them in your backpack.

BACKPA"C"K: _C_ommitment has to be in your backpack. In interviewing literally hundreds of people, I have discovered that people strive for excellence. But, I have also discovered that making a commitment is another story. Individuals are hesitant to make a full commitment to succeed. We need to encourage our youth to make a "commitment" to finish school, set goals, and always attempt to do their best. Once this commitment is made, they must understand that there can be no turning back to just being average; there is a necessity to strive for excellence.

BACKPAC"K": *K*eep on dreaming. Never – and I mean never – stop dreaming. It is our dreams that keep us focused and motivated to do whatever it takes to reach the next level. Nothing is impossible.

Allow me to share one of my dreams that I have put in my backpack. I have been a professional speaker for fourteen years, in the last seven years I have been blessed to have presented in over 350 schools. My new goal is to present in over 5,000 schools. Wow! I have a little way to go, don't I? I look forward to continually making a difference in the lives of our youth.

Let me encourage you to *never give up* on yourself, or on any of our youth. Never give up *hope*. Always remember, influence occurs in a single moment. We as parents and teachers have an awesome responsibility to discover that moment to influence every youth that crosses our paths.

My philosophy is, "Don't count what you have, but count what you have given, and that total equals your success." Pack your backpack of life with the right tools, and you will enjoy your journey to success. MUCHAS GRACIAS and God Bless.

Act Your Shoe Size, Not Your Age!

by
C. KEVIN WANZER

Act Your Shoe Size, Not Your Age!

by
C. KEVIN WANZER

A s a teacher, parent, or role model…you are a mentor. You know first hand that what an adult says to a young person can have a tremendous impact on his life. We all remember, as children, certain adults who encouraged us and helped shape our future. You may have even found yourself making quite a difference in a young person's life by a simple smile or word of praise. Unfortunately, not all adults are as positive and influential as you. However, as much as we try, we are not always purfect. Ooops. Every now and then we find ourselves slipping and saying things we swore we would never say as an adult.

Adults say the darndest things.

One time I was five years old (duh) and I was playing in a tree. My mom screamed, "Kevin, if you fall out of that tree and break both your legs…don't you come running to me!" Sound familiar?

My Dad used to proclaim, "This is going to hurt me, more than it is going to hurt you." I never understood that. I would reply, "Well then give me the paddle Dad and YOU turn around."

I would get so confused when my Mom would throw me for a loop. She would yell, "If I have told you once, I have told you a thousand times." Then seconds later, it was pop quiz time. "How many times have I told you?" she'd ask. I would just answer the question the best I could, "Ummm, a thousand and one?"

The truth is, there is no ideal way to raise a healthy productive young person. There is no instruction booklet or owners manual. However, if there was, perhaps it would be as simple as a brochure...

- Love them unconditionally.
- Encourage their youthful attitude toward life.
- Enhance their self-esteem by encouraging positive behavior.
- Praise their achievements.
- Provide them with safe alternatives to negative situations.

The list could go on and on. It is really pretty basic. If so, then why do so many adults have trouble grasping these relatively simple ideals.

Adults say the saddest things.

"Grow up." "When are you going to become a man?" "Why can't you be more mature?" "Be a little lady." "Stop acting like a child."

Why?

It seemed like when we were young and got into mischief or acted silly, we would hear from an adult, the same old, "Act your age, not your shoe size." What they actually meant was "Act *our* age." Sadly, some adults say they want young people to stay young as long as possible when in reality they want them to grow up and act like an adult as soon as possible.

The key word is act. This implies that some adults want young people to *act* like something they are *not*. Truth is, we should celebrate the way children act and hope that they maintain their disposition and attitude through life. In addition, we should encourage adults to remember the simplicities of childhood and try to act like children more often.

Think about it. Most children do not have a true concept of racism, sexism, homophobia, violence, handicaps and prejudice. Why does that change as some people age? We should challenge adults to act their shoe size, not their age.

Occasionally, I have the privilege of speaking in Hawaii. Hawaii is a different state...literally. Actually, it is a different state of mind. The mentality of Hawaiians is amazing. Most are unconditional toward others and accept all for who they are, not what they are. Hawaiians believe there are no adults...just different levels of childhood. What a wonderful concept.

That is my challenge to you...continue to cherish your sense of childlike wonderment as you begin to advance further into childhood. Your attitude can help teens maintain their positive outlook. Face it, there are thousands of statistics to measure how bad today's young generation is. But, it is difficult to measure why a young person chooses to make positive choices. You will never know for certain the lives you have touched. Your influence starts a cycle. The child you help will, in turn, help another.

Although I enjoy traveling and addressing thousands of young people and adults each year, I really am nothing out of the ordinary. I am just someone who was lucky enough to be exposed to a great deal of different experiences growing up. I never heard the words, "That is dumb. You can't grow up to do that." I was never discouraged from pursuing my dreams. As an adult now, it is easy to look back and find fault in my childhood...what I would have done differently if I were the parent. What is difficult is to look back and see what was done right.

I grew up in an abnormal home. Thank God. Notice I didn't say dysfunctional...we functioned...abnormally. My parents did it in their own unique way. My parents literally had a different language. To give you an idea, my Dad – and this is true – had different names for each of his knuckles. Honest to God. When he was younger he decided that it was sad that each knuckle had no identity of its own. Therefore, he took it upon himself to name his piekos (pronounced pee-eck-ohs) a.k.a. your knuckles. If you don't believe me, call him yourself. (Ask for Chuck.) He will be glad to name them for you...on his nose. Don't ask.

Needless to say, I grew up with a different perspective on life. Most of the time, my house was filled with laughter. I always chose to be drug-free and my parents were proud and supported my choice. I always knew that my parents appreciated my effort to be an individual. I learned early that life was made of cycles and to try to enjoy each one as much as possible.

When a child is playing with others and something does not go his way, he is likely to yell two very familiar words. "DO OVER!" These magical words stop action and as if to push the reset button, life starts from the beginning of whatever game they are playing. But life isn't made of DO OVERS. Or is it?

The Elementary Years
This is the cycle where attitudes develop.

In elementary school, success is measured on such simple terms: play fair, share, try everything on your plate. Happiness is achieved in such simple ways: blowing the seeds off a dandelion, chasing your shadow, petting a dog.

Status doesn't mean much. Or maybe it does. Slowly, young people become aware of what others have and have not. You try to behave and treat people nicely...doing what comes naturally. Kids know there are consequences for poor behavior: standing in the corner, putting your head down on your desk, writing "I will not lick the cat" a hundred times.

Regardless of their choices, the elementary cycle comes to an end. And they are awarded, sure enough, with the almighty DO OVER.

The Middle School Years
This is the cycle where attitudes become solid.

Suddenly, for some young people, they believe it is not acceptable to express their emotions...toward family, school or friends. Perhaps, they do want to show their desire to learn and better themselves. Some may feel embarrassed about getting good grades. The message I convey to a middle school student is "Don't apologize for your excellence. Never put yourself down for doing the right thing." If pre-teens can take pride in their decision to excel, then chances are they won't have to "pretend" to be something they are not.

How a young person feels at school relies greatly on how they feel at home. If self-esteem is not fully developed in a healthy way, middle school will be a tough battle. After all, a child will only feel as good as others around him will allow.

Eventually, the middle school years come to an end, too. Students know that their slate will be wiped clean. Because as they enter high school, sure enough, they get another DO OVER.

The High School Years

This is the cycle where attitudes can change with a lot of work.

High School is to prepare a young person for the inevitable real world. But maybe high school is more like the real world than you realize. The only big difference between high school and the real world is that in the real world, when you make bad choices, you don't have to go to detention hall. Or, maybe you do. Except this time it called prison. And I don't think you are allowed to put your head down on the desk.

It is evident that teenagers are already living in the real world and what they are about to face is insanity. Sure enough, the time comes for the inevitable DO OVER. Although, this time the next cycle lasts...forever.

If we look back at or own life cycles as children, it is amazing to see what we can learn from where we have been. We know there are no guarantees. As adults who empower teens, you do what you can to hold their hand as long as possible and hope they have the power to do what is right.

I believe young people want three things:
1) To have fun.
2) To have friends.
3) To do the right thing in life.

However, if you ask a young person to choose just two of the three, many will choose to have fun and have friends instead of doing the right thing. As mentors, we need to show that doing the right thing is not only possible...it is a necessity. Making positive choices in life, regardless of the consequences, is the lesson that must be taught.

This is much easier said than done. How do you possibly change the attitude of a person much less an entire student body? Here are some steps that might help:

• **Don't accept negative behaviors.**
There are certain behaviors and attitudes that are simply unacceptable in society. That message must be made loud and clear. Do not worry about alienating or offending a young person. Be a parent, teacher or mentor FIRST and a friend SECOND. Once the ground rules are established and adhered to, attitudes are destined to change for the better.

- **Start education early.**

Prejudice, violence or using alcohol and other drugs...are all learned behaviors. Unless education begins early, these cycles are destined to continue. To combat it an effective way, you must solve the problem before it ever starts.

- **Provide healthy alternatives.**

Young people need a place to call their own. As an adult, you need to continue to empower teens so that they can create the alternatives needed to resist destructive behavior.

- **Be an ally for all youth.**

Take a stand for the minorities of young people who need your support. Being a young person does not qualify one as a minority because a person eventually grows into adulthood. Being Jewish, gay, a person of color...those are true minorities. You are born and die with these characteristics. Any time an adult takes a stand for what is different, the life of a young person changes forever.

Being an adult who empowers teens is no easy task. Truth be told, if the teenager feels unconditional love from you, chances are they will admire and follow the steps you take. We simply must teach young people to choose to love.

choose to love

it is amazing in this world today
filled with love and hate
what separates the common man
from the man who is truly great

it is not the wealth in his bank account
or the possessions in his own back yard
but it is instead, what he keeps inside
of his loving, understanding heart

you do not choose to be born black or white
you don't choose to be born rich or poor
you do not choose to be deaf or blind
wishing you had something more

you do not choose to be straight or gay
you don't choose to be woman or man
you do not choose the family of yours
it's all part of God's great plan

and although for some it's hard to relate,
to the differences others endure,
keep in mind that their are some choices
that make you shallow or pure

you do choose to love or hate
you do choose to follow or lead
you do choose to embrace or ignore
others, in their time of need

some things in life you cannot alter
but your attitude can change, it's true
and by doing so you can affect
the people who look up to you

the meaning of life is the greatest mystery of all
but the answer is easily found
it is unconditional love for all mankind
who walk on our common ground

Like most things, change will not happen overnight. Simply continue to do what you can…day by day…week by week…year by year…and you will see a change for the better.

525,600 Minutes

Recently, I saw the Tony award-winning Broadway show *Rent*. It was amazing. In it, there is a song titled "Seasons of Love." It discusses how people measure the length of one year. "In sunrises, in sunsets, in midnight's, in cups of coffee…." It really got me thinking. The simplest messages sometimes are the most difficult to comprehend. Some people are preoccupied about getting older. They measure their life merely in years. What if we had no concept of years? What if we measured our lives in the number of people we have touched in a positive way? Imagine that. We would actually want to be as old as possible as soon as possible.

I realize that the fact you are even reading this book (and chances are you are reading this right now), shows that you are not the typical adult. You are already making choices that help the lives of young people on a daily basis. You are a true ally for today's young people. Critics would even claim that I am only preaching to the choir. But as the adage goes, "If the choir doesn't sing, than nobody is going to sing."

So, when another "adult" challenges you about your behavior with young people, or questions whether or not what you are doing really makes a difference, instead of arguing with them, feel pity. Obviously they do not understand. They are not as old as you. Not in years…but in the lives you've touched. And when they look at you cautiously and question, "How old are you anyway?" You can proudly look at them and say, "I lost count in the millions." Then smile and walk away.

After all, it is not your age in years that matters, it is maintaining the age of your attitude throughout your entire life. And if you ever forget how old you are attitude wise, just glance toward your feet. Act your shoe size. Not your age.

(By the way, I am an 11 and a half. But I am still growing. I hope to someday be a size 10.)

Chapter

13

Thank You!

by
Ty Sells

TEEN
POWER

Thank You!

by
TY SELLS

Thank you. It just doesn't seem like enough. We see celebrities making an attempt to appreciate the little people on all of the award shows, and no matter how sincere they may be, they just never seem to get it right. Thank you is just two small words trying to convey a huge and abstract feeling. A feeling that embodies joy, relief, security, gratitude, etc., etc., etc. My second grade teacher Mrs. Marcum taught me to read and write and what does she get back from me? Thank you. Mrs. Hussey explained to me that fifth graders, myself included, were just as important as everyone else in the world, and all I have for her is thank you. Father Lutz let me know that asking questions and challenging inconsistencies is not only acceptable, but also necessary. Guess what he gets in return – good guess, a heaping helping of thank you. And thanks is what I offer any adult that is reading this book, working to influence young people in positive ways.

As parents, mentors, and adult advisors, you're participating in the most awesome and rewarding job of our time. Along with this task comes a great deal of responsibility. This responsibility can be intimidating. You may find yourself questioning your abilities at times, saying things like, "Can I really make a difference?" "Do I have enough energy to work with kids?" or "I wonder if people know I talk to myself?" These are all great questions, especially the last one. It is my hope to reassure you that by simply possessing the desire to work with young people and by searching out resources, like this book, to make sure you are doing a good job, you already have what it takes.

I have been working with young people for over 10 years (as a matter of fact, I used to be a young person) with a program known as Youth to Youth International. I have already had to deal with a number of the questions and doubts you may currently be struggling with. I certainly do not claim to know all of the answers. Actually I only have a few answers, like six answers really, and those are true and false answers. I mean you could probably guess those – I am sorry, I seemed to have lost focus. Where was I? Oh yeah, I just hope my experiences can help. Often to find success for ourselves, we should examine the success of others.

Many times adults claim to have *"lost touch"* with today's youth. Now, there are a few kinds of *"lost touch."* One is you no longer feel that you are speaking the same language as the young ones. You don't understand their clothing, music and hairstyles. And their dancing frightens you and makes you turn away in shame and embarrassment. This is the type of *"lost touch"* we will be talking about.

The other has something to do with hearing voices in your head, constantly murmuring nursery rhymes, and doing what some may call a *"happy dance."*

We must first establish if you, as an adult, have *"lost touch"* with the youth of today. Here is a quiz to help you find out. Please answer yes or no to the following questions.

1. Have you recently bragged, "Hey, look I finally got the Macarena?"

2. Do you think Tommy, Abercrombie and Calvin are the Three Stooges: The Next Generation?

3. Did you think Ellen's "coming out," had something to do with six more weeks of winter?

4. It has been more than several months since the publishing of this book and these questions still have relevance to you.

If you answered yes to any or all of these questions, you may be on your way to losing touch. **Congratulations!** You see, being in touch with young people is less important than being in touch with yourself. Gaining touch with young people requires you to know your own values, interests, and talents. By sharing more of your self, you will get more from them in return. You don't need to be a part of their posse, or even know that "Phat" isn't an insult. You need to know that you care about youth and more importantly, they need to know you care about them.

Genuinely caring about these people is the only constant. Caring will get you through every challenge and augment every reward. Without caring, working with youth is an exercise in futility. Along with caring, here is a quick list of Do's and Don'ts that may help.

DO –

- **Trust your youth!** Allow the youth that you are working with to make decisions regarding the direction of their future. They may know the fastest and most direct way of reaching their goals. Their ideas are gold!

- **Get to know the youth personally!** This personal contact is the most important link of a successful relationship. It's often difficult to buy into an idea or concept, without first buying into the person sharing it. Once you have invested personally, their reason to succeed becomes personal.

- **Trust yourself!** Often adults are intimidated to work with youth. Trust that your ability stems from your desire to help.

- **Treat youth with respect!** Age is just a measuring tool. No one likes to be "yelled at" or "talked down to." You'll find that from 5 to 95 we all like to be respected.

- **Be flexible!** Random and chaotic. These are terms that are associated with today's youth. They are also the way successful youth programs may appear to the untrained eye. It is important to capture the attention and imagination of the youth you serve. Adaptability is necessary.

- **Practice what you preach!** 'Nuf said.

DON'T –

- **Save the world!** Because you are working with youth, you obviously care about what is going on in our world. Remain focused on your group and the individuals within it. Doing your best to help them is a big enough challenge. When they start helping others, then the world will take care of itself.

- **Be an expert!** The most important thing you can do is to continue learning. Youth, colleagues, parents, and other adults, are all great resources for new ideas. Being open to other resources, allows for the most opportunity for success.

- **Protect them from mistakes!** Making mistakes is an outstanding way to learn. Life's experiences is the greatest teacher. Your job is to protect them from harm and make sure they are not afraid to make other mistakes.

- **Forget what it was like to be young!** "That'll never work." "You're too young to understand." These are the comments that make us cynical and limit our vision. Embrace their desire to make their world a better place.

I am aware at this point many of you may be thinking that a great deal of this information is common sense or at least fundamental. I would completely agree with you. You see, I believe that if more people took a common sense approach to life, the world would be a happier and healthier place. We sometimes try to complicate things instead of focusing on the basics.

Keys are a basic necessity for day to day functioning. I use keys to get in my house, car, office, filing cabinet, and many other necessary things. I could not get around without my keys. Without keys I would lose my job, shelter, and freedom. Yet every other day, I seem to misplace them. And this is not just a small ring with two or three keys, this is the big key ring with like 940 keys. The kind a janitor might carry. The kind that if you carry them around too much, you could develop back problems. The kind you are not supposed to operate after taking some medications. The kind that Schwarzenegger says, "No way I'm lifting those!" The kind – well you get the picture, my keys are not easy to misplace.

The point is that I routinely lose something that is incredibly basic and important to my daily existence. I run around the house frantically flipping couch pillows, and checking places I've never even seen before. The whole time yelling to my wife, "Honey, have you seen my keys?" By the time I'm about to start my second lap around the house, frantically searching places I've already checked, my wife, Angie, stops me and tells me to calm down. She then says, "Your keys are right where you left them." At first, this seems like a sarcastic comment that is meant to mock and tease me. But I quickly realize she is right. I stop and remember the last time I had the keys. I then retrace my steps from that point until I find them.

This often happens when adults work with young people. In our effort to influence, perfect or evaluate, we complicate the process and often lose sight of the basics. We lose the **KEYS** to working with youth.

Knowledge is the first key. As I stated earlier, an adult must know why they are working with young people. They must also get to know what rewards they receive from working with youth, and what do they have to offer the youth. This knowledge will help when finding common interests or shared experiences with young people.

Energy and enthusiasm are the next keys. Energy begets energy. If adults demonstrate excitement about opportunities to work with youth, the youth will be excited about working with adults. Advisors, mentors and parents must also celebrate the success, no matter how small, a young person enjoys.

You control your image. This third key is often overlooked. The image you should convey to young people is yourself. Don't get caught up in being cool, or a best friend. Be your self, be consistent and be honest. That is what young people want from adults. By practicing what you preach, your message becomes more clear and attainable for others.

Shampoo instructions. Lather, rinse, and repeat. The repeat part is what is crucial. Once you have experienced some level of success, continue to practice the fundamental, common sense, **KEYS** which brought you to that point.

Never lose sight of these **KEYS**. They are far too valuable to misplace. **K**nowledge, **E**nergy, **Y**our Image, and **S**hampoo Instructions will offer you access to far more valuable places than cars and filing cabinets. They will allow you access into the hearts and minds of today's youth.

A Chinese proverb was taught to me when I was a young boy. This adaptation of the proverb reminds us of the importance of our **KEYS**. I think more than any other story it most clearly teaches the value and importance of working with young people. This story reminds us of why we do what we do. And at the same time asks us to keep doing it.

Once upon a time, there was a rich and powerful emperor. He was a kind and benevolent ruler, who presided over the most beautiful kingdom in the entire world. The only problem was no one outside the kingdom ever got to enjoy its beauty. This was because the kingdom was deep in the Dark Forest and there were no roads that led into the forest. This troubled the emperor, so he decided to build a new road. This would be the most incredible road ever, and would allow people from all over to come and enjoy his perfect kingdom.

Upon completion of the new road, the emperor announced that he was going to hold a huge party to celebrate this joyous occasion. He invited people from all over the world to travel the new road and come and join him in the celebration.

As an incentive, he announced that whoever traveled the road the best would receive an award of $50,000. This challenge was well received and thousands of people, from all over, traveled the road as well as they could. Some drove fancy cars, some jogged in tuxedos, others crawled on their hands and knees, and still others hovered over the road in hang gliders.

As each individual arrived at the kingdom, the emperor greeted them. "How do you like my new road?" he asked. Each person responded without fail, "It is the most beautiful road I have ever traveled. Lovely hills, smooth pavement, and nice curves. It was perfect, except for the one pile of rock and debris left over from construction. After swerving around that I noticed no other flaws." The emperor thanked each person and welcomed him or her into the kingdom. He said, "I will be announcing the award winner later, please enjoy the party until then."

Hours passed and the crowd became restless. They repeatedly asked, "Who traveled the road the best? Who won the $50,000?" The emperor simply said, "I am not yet ready to announce the best traveler. Please continue enjoying the party."

Finally, as the crowd was completely frustrated, a man stumbled through the kingdom gates. His shirt was torn, his hair was messy, he had blood on his arm, and he was completely exhausted. In his left hand was a burlap sack. The emperor greeted him and asked, "How did you like my new road?" The exhausted man answered, "It is the most beautiful and perfect road I have ever seen." Asked the emperor, "If it is so perfect, why are you so late?" The man responded, "Well, there was one pile of rock and debris left over from construction. I decided to move the pile so no one would get hurt. By the way, I found this sack filled with $50,000, it must be yours." The emperor corrected the man, "This sack of money is yours. You win the award because you traveled the road the best. You traveled it the best because you made it easier for those coming after you."

Who has made the road easier for you? Maybe whoever constructed this confusing crazy world we live in knew that thank you would never seem like enough. Maybe the only real way to repay the people who have made our roads easier, is to continue on, constantly clearing the debris left by others. As teachers, parents, drug prevention specialists and adult advisors, we must remind ourselves that our payment doesn't come by reaching a destination, but by helping others to travel the road.

I personally can not begin to count the people who have made my road easier. I only hope that by continuing to work with young people, my actions will one day adequately demonstrate all the appreciation I feel from their efforts. Until that time, however, thank you will just have to do. So to all of my teachers, aunts and uncles, thank you. To my adult advisors and mentors, thanks. And Mom and Dad – well, I think you know how I feel.

Who Wrote What
and Why –
Meet the Authors

TEEN
POWER

BOBBY PETROCELLI

Making a Difference...10 Seconds at a Time!

"Working with youth is not a stepping stone for some greater calling, <u>it is the greatest calling!</u>"

Bobby Petrocelli is a former teacher, guidance counselor. His zest for life and sincere love for youth is communicated through his message. Those who experience Bobby leave motivated by his awesome story and refreshed by his charismatic personality. As he combines his expertise and riveting personal experience, Bobby never fails to inspire, empower and encourage. He travels internationally sharing his great news to all ages, from all walks of life, in his own enthusiastic energetic and humorous way!

10 Seconds, Inc.
P.O. Box 2411
Chesapeake, VA 23327
757-547-7162 (Phone & Fax)
800-547-7933
tseconds@erols.com

Bobby is the author of <u>Triumph Over Tragedy,</u> and has co-authored the book <u>Teen Power Too</u> and has been featured in many magazines, newspapers, television and radio programs. Bobby lives in Virginia with his incredible wife Suzy, and their two awesome sons, Alec and Aron (Who look just like their Daddy!).

SANDY QUEEN

The Power of the Dream

Sandy is the Founder and Director of Lifeworks, Inc., a training/consulting firm in Columbia, Maryland, that specializes in helping people take a better look at their lives though humor, laughter and play. She has developed many innovative programs in the areas of stress reduction, humor, children's wellness and self esteem.

Sandy is known throughout the U.S., Canada and Australia as a dynamic lecturer, humorist and educator with a special focus on children and those who work with children, but most important, a focus on the child within each of us.

LIFEWORKS
P.O. Box 2668
Columbia, MD 21045-1668
410-992-7665 fax 964-9036
goodstf@aol.com

Sandy speaks with inspiration and humor. Her philosophy – LIGHTEN UP! THIS IS THE ONLY LIFE YOU HAVE!

She is a mother, grandmother, humorist, writer and trainer; but most of all – a person interested in and dedicated to helping people develop a sense of their own uniqueness.

ERIC CHESTER, CSP

The "Why" Factor – *How to Keep Teens on Your Team!*

As a former high school teacher and coach, a nationally recognized youth motivational speaker and author, and the parent of four kids between the ages of 12 and 17, Eric Chester really knows how to EmPower Teens. His entertaining keynotes and workshops provide both the *"want to"* and the *"how to"* for thousands of parents and educators each year. His popular program *"From Creature to Teacher to Reacher"* has become a favorite for staff development meetings world-wide, and parent groups love Eric's address *"Bridging the Gap."* Eric is the player-coach of the popular <u>Teen Power</u> book series.

c/o TEEN POWER
1410 Vance St. - Ste. #201
Lakewood, CO 80215
303-239-9999 fax 239-9901
800-304-ERIC
ECSpeak@aol.com
www.ericchester.com

JOHN CRUDELE, CSP

Funhouse or Madhouse?
Becoming Love's Reflection

Throughout the past 14 years, John's presented over 3,000 programs to more than one million people internationally. Popular with students and adults, John impacts school, conference and community audiences with life-changing messages, humorous insights and a powerful delivery style. His books *Making Sense of Adolescence: How to Parent From the Heart*, and his contributions to the *TEEN POWER* series unravel the mysteries of adolescence. He is a frequent guest on talk-radio and TV shows including the *Rikki Lake* and *Jenny Jones* shows. Youth and parent cassette programs are also available.

John Crudele
Speeches and Seminars
9704 Yukon Court
Minneapolis, MN 55438
612-942-6207 fax 942-7601
800-899-9KID
JCSpeak@aol.com

Scott Friedman, CSP

Chalk One Up For Laughter

A motivational humorist, Scott Friedman gets your audience laughing. . .and skillfully slips in plenty of practical ideas on overcoming stress, conquering burnout, and making change work. While tickling funny bones with a quick wit and playful style, Scott is opening minds to new ideas. Participants leave feeling better about themselves, their careers, and their futures.

Scott holds a degree in marketing and psychology from Southern Methodist University. He served on the DECA Advisory Board for Cherry Creek High School in Colorado. Scott twice served as President of the Colorado Speakers Association and earned the Certified Speaking Professional designation from the National Speakers Association.

Scott Friedman & Associates
1563 South Trenton Court
Denver, CO 80231
303-671-7222 fax 368-5781
FunnyScott@aol.com
www.scott-friedman.com

Michael Scott Karpovich, CSP

Life Is Never Fair

Diagnosed with brain damage at age four, beaten up and called a "nerd" by bullies... this unlikely hero has discovered that our greatest adversities are what really make us strong! Michael has worked successfully as a farmer, a popular disc jockey, a high school drama coach, a counselor and a college instructor! Described as half Robin Williams and half Leo Buscaglia, Michael speaks to over 300,000 people annually, is the youngest president of the Professional Speakers Association of Michigan, and is one of less than 300 Certified Speaking Professionals on the planet! (Not bad for a brain-damaged nerd!)

P. O. Box 272
Caro, MI 48723-0272
fax 517-673-0116
800-718-3367
karpovich@aol.com
www.karpovich.com

MILTON L. CREAGH

Do You Hear What They're Saying?
Do You Hear What They're Feeling?

Milton L. Creagh is an internationally known drug prevention speaker for conferences, conventions, assembly programs, youth rallies and workshops. He speaks to more than half a million people annually.

Milton is host of the critically acclaimed, national PBS television series, "Parenting Works!" This upbeat, humorous talk show is designed to help parents deal with real life situations.

Milton is also co-author and host of the new docu-drama, "MASQUERADE: Unveiling Our Deadly Dance With Drugs and Alcohol." Milton's work has also been chronicled on such television programs as "Screen Scene" (Black Entertainment Television /BET); "Fox on the Family" (FOX News Network / FNN); and "Turner Entertainment Report" (Turner Broadcasting Service /TBS).

Milton Creagh & Associates
P. O. Box 830126
Stone Mountain, GA 30083
770-981-9113 fax 981-5160

BILL CORDES

FAITH is Not a Four Letter Word

"Bill Cordes is not really a person, he's an experience."

His experience will lead you down the path of "Participation is the...Key." Since 1988, he has provided experiences for corporations, teachers and students on 100's of high school and college campuses. He has keynoted numerous state and national programs for FBLA, FFA, FHA, DECA, PBL, VICA, BACCHUS/GAMMA, STUCO, NCCLS, and many other important organizations. In his programs you are likely to scale mountains of optimism, and slide down trails of possibilities. Since he is nationwide, he is everywhere you want to be, so bring your Mastermind because he won't take anything from Negative Express.

Cordes Keynotes & Seminars
2920 Quivira
Great Bend, KS 67530
316-793-7227 fax 793-5024
800-401-6670
YOGOWYPI@aol.com

CLARE LaMERES

Failure: Breakfast of Champions

LaMeres Lifestyles Unlimited
P.O. Box 8326
Newport Beach, CA 92658
714-854-2683 fax 854-5695

Responsible, motivated, caring, achievement-oriented students? Enthusiastic, energetic, competent, dedicated teachers? The stuff of fantasy? Not according to Clare LaMeres, one of the world's most sought after presenters. These students and teachers exist <u>everywhere</u> and Clare teaches you how to multiply them in her fast-paced, enjoyable, highly practical keynote addresses and seminars. Clare has authored <u>The Winner's Circle: Yes I Can! Self Esteem Lessons for the Secondary Classroom</u>. Her successful strategies are being used in over one million classrooms and teacher education courses throughout North America, Europe and Taiwan. The most oft-repeated evaluation of her presentations: *"Every teacher and parent in America should hear Clare speak!"*

BOB LENZ

Foundations For Life

"I don't want to see young people cheated out of life."

LIFE Promotions
213 E. College Ave.
Appleton, WI 54911-5712
fax 414-738-5587
800-955-LIFE (5433)
LifePromotions@juno.com

Each year Bob speaks to 100,000 youth and adults across North America with messages of hope, courage and respect. He quickly connects with his audiences through powerful stories, experiences and humor moving them from laughter to tears. The result? They leave with a message they won't soon forget.

Since 1982, Bob Lenz has reached teens through school assemblies, conferences and church groups.

Although Bob loves speaking, his first commitment is to his wife, Carol and their five children.

JIMMY CABRERA, CSP

Packing for Success
Preparing for the Future

Getting "MAD!" Yes, "Making A Difference" is what Jimmy is all about. As a professional speaker, his messages have been heard by over one million individuals in the past 14 years. In the last 8 years, Jimmy has presented in over 350 schools, including all grade levels. He is dynamic and energetic, riveting his audience's attention through the very last sentence. Every presentation is his unique blend of motivation and education. He sees the need for communication, education, and positive influence in our culturally interdependent society. Call or write for more information on Jimmy's availability.

Success Through Excellence, Inc.
1827 Roanwood Drive
Houston, TX 77090
281-537-0032 fax 537-9242
800-437-ICAN(4226)
JimmySpeaks@Juno.com

C. KEVIN WANZER

Act Your Shoe Size, Not Your Age!

As an adult, Kevin Wanzer is still in high school. Well, not just high school. Actually schools of all grades. An honors graduate of Butler University in Indianapolis, Kevin travels to quite a few schools as he takes his student audiences on an outrageous and electrifying journey. While his message of personal excellence, drug education and prejudice might not be unique; his presentations to schools, educators, parents, and adults will definitely be remembered. Kevin dedicates his chapter to all those who empowered him as a teen and to those who continue to empower today's teens...especially one of the greatest teachers of all, Christopher Martz. Mahalo.

P.O. Box 30384
Indianapolis, IN 46230-0384
317-253-4242
800-4.KEVIN.W
justsayha@aol.com
http://members.aol.
com/justsayha

Ty Sells

Thank You!

Ty cares deeply for the well-being of youth. Known for his charisma, humor and leadership; he has been speaking professionally since 1992, presenting to hundreds of school assemblies and conference keynotes throughout the world including the U.S. Canada, Bermuda, Cayman Islands and Italy. Not only a speaker, Ty has over ten years experience in drug prevention and community service.

Training Manager
Youth to Youth International
700 Bryden Road, Third Floor
Columbus, OH 43215
614-224-4506 fax 224-8451
Y2YINT@NETSET.COM

Ty is also the Training Manager for Youth to Youth International, a proven leader in the field of youth development and drug prevention. Youth to Youth provides conferences, training and consultation for the enhancement of teen leadership skills.

Other
TEEN POWER

Books Available Through ChesPress

TEEN POWER *A Treasury of Solid Gold Advice for Today's Teens* from America's Top Youth Speakers, Trainers, and Authors.

TEEN POWER TOO *More Solid Gold Advice for Teens* from America's Top Speakers, Trainers, and Authors.

PreTEEN POWER *A Treasury of Solid Gold Advice for Those Just Entering Their Teens* from America's Top Youth Speakers, Trainers, and Authors.

Need a
sensational speaker?

**Want information about other Teen Power
books and materials?**

**Like to find out about upcoming
Teen Power conferences and events?**

**— Perhaps you'd just like to get
a quick, motivational
"HOT THOUGHT"**

Have we got a 'site' for you. . .

www.teenpower.com